PUBLIC
OPINION AND
CONTEMPORARY
DISARRAY

WITHDRAWN

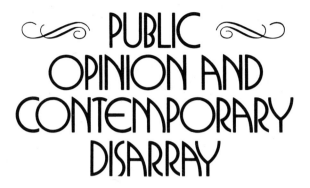

PUBLIC OPINION AND CONTEMPORARY DISARRAY

RICHARD E. DAWSON
Washington University

HARPER & ROW, PUBLISHERS
New York, Evanston, San Francisco, London

Sponsoring Editor: Walter H. Lippincott, Jr.
Project Editor: Eleanor Castellano
Designer: June Negrycz
Production Supervisor: Robert A. Pirrung

Library of Congress Cataloging in Publication Data
Dawson, Richard E
    PUBLIC OPINION AND CONTEMPORARY DISARRAY.
    1.   United States—Politics and government—1969-
2. Public opinion—United States. I. Title.
E855.D35   301.15'43'3209730924   73-6228
ISBN 0-06-041596-7

For Karen

CONTENTS

PREFACE

This book offers a description of contemporary American political opinions. It identifies the key policy concerns of the American public, analyzes the distributions of opinions regarding current political and social issues, and suggests how the contemporary patterns of issue saliency and opinion distributions affect the current political climate. The central argument of the book is that there have been important shifts over the past decade in the issue focus of American politics and alterations in the structural distribution of political opinions. Several new issue areas have emerged as key policy concerns for much of the public. New patterns of conflict and consensus have developed in response to these shifts in issue saliency. These new conflicts divide the population in patterns that differ from those associated with the key issue concerns of previous decades. They cut through many of the economic, social, demographic, and political groupings that structured political life in the immediate past. They contribute to what we call the current state of political disarray. These new issues and the accompanying disarray have made it difficult for political leadership to respond very effectively to contemporary political interests and demands.

The central focus and key concerns of this book have emerged from several years of teaching courses on public opinion and American politics. The book is a part of more extensive research on changes over time in the conditions that structure opinion distributions in American society. The focus on opinion distributions has been influenced by the work of K. O. Key, Jr., especially his *Public Opinion and American Democracy,* published more than a decade ago. Although the analysis developed here goes off into different directions from those of Key, the importance of analyzing how opinion distributions are structured and how one might look at these relationships were lessons learned from reading Key's work and using it in the teaching of public opinion.

The thinking and research that have gone into this essay have been developed over several years. The author has received assistance in this

work from a number of sources. A Ford Foundation Faculty Research
Fellowship for the academic year 1968–1969 aided in the initial
thinking and preliminary research out of which the book developed.
Much of the specific data analysis reported on here and the draft of the
original manuscript were accomplished under the auspicies of a
National Science Foundation Grant (Grant No. GS-3168) during the
1970–1971 academic year. The grant provided time off from teaching
responsibilities for the author, helped fund the data acquisition and
analysis, and provided important research assistance. The author wishes
to acknowledge the contributions of both the Ford Foundation and the
National Science Foundation and to thank them for their assistance.

For the most part the discussion and analysis presented in this book
are based on national public opinion polls and survey research data. The
data used were collected by several different survey research organizations. The bulk of the analysis is based on the election studies
conducted by the University of Michigan Survey Research Center. The
SRC survey data were made available through the Inter-University
Consortium for Political Research. In addition to the SRC studies data
collected by the American Institute of Public Opinion (Gallup Poll),
Roper Polls, and the National Opinion Research Center are used in the
analysis. Most of the data from these three research agencies were
obtained from the Roper Public Opinion Research Center, located at
Williams College. They were made available through the International
Survey Library Association. The Roper Center and its staff were very
helpful in assisting the author in locating particular types of data and in
providing both data sets and some basic data analysis. Still other data
were taken from *The Gallup Opinion Index*, a monthly publication put
out by Gallup International, Inc. I try to make clear the exact sources
of the data as they are presented in the text.

This research would not have been possible without the availability
of survey data collected by these various organizations and dis-
seminated through the Inter-University Consortium and the International Library Association of the Roper Center. The fact that we now
have more than thirty-five years of national sample survey data
available and the existence of organizations that make the data readily
available to students and scholars make feasible a wide variety of
research on public opinion.

The preparation of this book and the research on which it is based have been aided by a number of students, several of whom merit special acknowledgement here. Ronald Gilson aided the author in the earliest stage of the research and thinking that have gone into this book. Fred Teitelbaum carried out the bulk of the computer data analysis which serves as the basis for the discussion. Roger Lowery assisted with data analysis in the later stages of the research. Ronald Satnick read an early draft of the manuscript and made useful comments many of which are incorporated in the final text.

Two colleagues, Kenneth Prewitt and David Greenstone, both of the University of Chicago, read an early draft of the manuscript and made useful suggestions with respect to organization and presentation of the argument. I would like to acknowledge their assistance and offer them my special thanks.

R.E.D.

PUBLIC
OPINION AND
CONTEMPORARY
DISARRAY

CHAPTER 1
PUBLIC OPINION AND POLITICAL DISARRAY

At the beginning of the 1970s much in American political life appears in a state of flux, of general disarray. Curious new patterns of conflict and consensus, of change and nonchange, of questioning and certitude have emerged to create a disquieting political mood. The peaceful apathy of the 1950s, the hopeful and active years of the early and mid-1960s have given way to feelings of doubt, impatience, frustration, and intense conflicts. Much of the "conventional wisdom" or traditional notions about American politics has been confounded by an impressive string of events and alterations. The past decade has seen a series of political assassinations,[1] widespread use of demonstrations and acts of violence for the expression of political interests and demands, and the formation of new politically conscious groups. The aggressive activists among the minority poor, student radicals drawn largely from high-income families, "hard hat" union members, and traditionally liberal ethnic groups taking up the conservative banner to fight against social and economic changes represent a few of these new groups. These changes challenge not only many of the understandings and myths through which the average citizen has viewed his politics but also many of the conceptualizations and interpretations of the political analyst. Much that has been said in the recent past about stability, orderliness, legitimacy, efficaciousness, and widespread consensus in American political life has come to appear quite vulnerable.

This book is an attempt to bring into better perspective some aspects of this political disarray and disquiet by focusing on the political opinions of Americans. It seeks to portray and to analyze the substance, structure, and distribution of contemporary political opinions as a means of developing a partial description and explanation of the current political change and uneasiness. A major theme is that newly developing patterns of opinion distributions do not relate systematically to the traditional instruments of political expression and representation (e.g., political parties, representative bodies, and elections). This lack of tie-in makes it difficult for government to respond rapidly and effectively to new political demands. Likewise, it renders it difficult for the citizenry to express concerns through normal channels.

The relationships between the opinions, interests, and values of the citizenry, on the one hand, and the policies and operations of their government, on the other hand, have been important and enduring foci of political analysis. Normative theorists have offered varying prescriptions as to whether and to what extent governmental forms and actions should be determined by popular opinion. Empirical analysts have focused on the extent to which public policy does, or does not, follow public opinion (and vice versa, how public opinion often follows government policy) and the consequences of different types of opinion distributions for the operation of the political system.

Some of the central political concerns of the present period of discontent are tied in closely with issues pertaining to the relationship between government and the public. One of the key slogans of those seeking to change or to disavow government policies has been the assertion that people must be permitted to influence and to participate in the making of decisions which affect their lives. Although this theme has been most closely associated with the student left, the militant poor, and the disadvantaged minorities, these groups are not the only ones to take up the demand for more citizen participation. Middle-class citizens, who are unhappy with the policies adopted by local school boards or other governmental bodies, have been found voicing similar sentiments in demanding that public officials respond to their desires. They are pressing in a similar vein for greater citizen involvement in the making of policies. Union members, who are unhappy with policies pertaining to racial equality or race quotas in jobs, argue similarly as they protest governmental policies.

From the outset, one of the key issues in the dispute over U.S. involvement in Southeast Asia centered around the relationship between public opinion and various aspects of the war effort. On the one hand, there was the question of whether or not the involvement has or has not had popular support. On the other hand, there has been the question of the extent to which policies and activities such as the Vietnam conflict should be directly reflective of public opinion. It might be that as far as domestic politics are concerned, relationships between the government and the public—such things as the attempts of leaders to manipulate and sometimes to mislead public opinion, the withholding of information concerning the course of the war, and the frustrations felt by many who have sought unsuccessfully to influence the course of the conflict—may be more significant than the actual outcome in Southeast Asia.

Three basic conditions in contemporary American political life seem to underlie and help give shape to the current sense of political malaise. First, the last few years have witnessed the rise of a growing disquiet, and even a sense of frustration, among many people. This disquiet has been associated with alterations in basic opinion relationships and with the breakup of some of the social and political coalitions that have given meaning and structure to political life over the past few decades. There is a sense of change or pressure for change, but a lack of focus and structure to the various pressures. This condition we refer to as political disarray. Second, the disquiet and disarray are related to alterations in the focus of political concerns. There have been changes in the types of issues that are most salient to the public and in the socioeconomic conditions and groupings that structure political outlooks and consequently political conflict and consensus. Third, these important changes in issue focus and in the conditions that structure political interests and outlooks have rendered it difficult for political institutions such as political parties, representative bodies, and the electoral process to respond very clearly and effectively to much of what people are most concerned with. The shifts in issue and policy concerns, the emergence of new groupings and coalitions, and the uncertainty and confusion of much of the citizenry have made it difficult for political leaders to address many present-day concerns clearly.

Indicators of political disquiet and disarray are plentiful and readily identifiable. A few will be mentioned to suggest the substance and scope of what is being referred to here. The politicization and mobilization of groups such as college students, blacks, hard hats, and veterans; the use of rallies, demonstrations, and the take-over of public buildings to voice political concerns and protests; the incidences of politically motivated acts of violence (assassinations, bombings, arson, etc.) are, of course, the most notorious examples of unrest and frustration. Other factors, less dramatic but maybe with greater long-range impact, also testify to this disquiet. Among these are shifts in electoral behavior and partisan attachment, shifts that seem to indicate growing disaffection with political processes and institutions.

The last three presidential elections have seen a decline of some magnitude in voter turnout. Outside the South there was a decrease of 8.2 percent in the turnout rate for presidential voting between 1960 and 1968.[2] In 1960 the turnout rate reached a twentieth-century high point of 71.9 percent. By 1968 it had fallen to 63.7 percent. In 1972 the turnout rate was even lower. Although some political analysts have argued that low voting rates indicate a satisfied citizenry, one that does not want change, this hardly seems to be the case at the present time. It seems more accurate to view this decrease in turnout rate for voting as an indication of dissatisfaction with some aspects of the process of political and electoral choice.

Public opinion polls have reported a decrease in the incidence of political party identification. The number of persons declining to identify with either of the two major parties has increased substantially over the past decade. In 1969, for the first time since systematic sample surveys began gauging party preferences there were more persons who called themselves Independents than identifiers with the smaller of the two parties, the Republicans. These changes can be seen even more dramatically in changes over time in responses to a question posed in Gallup polls as to whether or not the respondent would choose today to register as a Republican, a Democrat, or an Independent. Between 1960 and 1971 the number of Democratic identifiers increased by 21 percent, the number of Republican identifiers decreased by 5 percent, while the number of Independents increased by 326 percent. At the same time the number of potential voters increased by 27 percent. In 1960 those choosing Independent represented 6 percent of the sample. In 1971 they constituted 19 percent.[3] The tendency not to identify with either of the major parties is particularly high among the young. A Gallup Poll taken in 1970 reports that slightly over half of the college students reported having no party identification.[4] Some political analysts see a major party realignment at hand. Others suggest that parties may be becoming less important in shaping our political life. Regardless of what may happen to the parties in the long run, it seems that the singificant decrease in party identification, coupled with the decrease in voting and the use of less conventional avenues of political expression and protest, indicate a sense of political disquiet that is both deep and widespread.

The confusion and disarray of the present political situation are also indicated by strange new alliances and political associations that are emerging across the political terrain. In the past few years normally Democratic labor leaders have turned up for political dinners and speeches of the Republican vice president, Spiro Agnew. Agnew at the same time is a favorite of the Republican right, the traditional political enemy of most organized labor. The labor leaders applaud the vice president's outspoken stand on demonstrations and on law and order. Among the most vocal opponents of the establishment and the status quo are the sons and daughters of wealthier citizens. These youthful dissidents often attend the most prestigious colleges and universities and under "normal" circumstances would be heading for careers in the most privileged positions in society. Both political commentators and the general public have come to view the industrial workers and the "ethnics" as most likely to be conservatives in the contemporary struggles over social and economic change. Only a few years ago these same groups generally were viewed as forming the bulk of the liberals—those supporting changes in social, economic, and political relationships. Large numbers of those with high incomes and prestigious positions in business and the professions have become prominent advocates of current liberal causes such as support for more government intervention in behalf of minorities, opposition to U.S. involvement in Southeast Asia, and even advocates of expanding federal welfare services. In the decades of the thirties, forties, and fifties, programs involving greater governmental participation in social and economic relationships received little support from the wealthier and more privileged.

Many of the traditional categories, images, labels, and relationships that have been used to give meaning and order to American political life do not fit the contemporary political world. The economic groupings, ethnic associations, and ideological outlooks which developed around the issues of economic security during the Depression and New Deal years, and which have served to give structure to parties, elections, and political preferences in subsequent decades, have become less relevant for the current age. New categories, new images, and new relationships have not yet emerged with clarity and stability—hence, the state of confusion and disarray.

One of the key factors creating this disarray is a shift in problem focus or issue saliency. During the past decade new issues have become salient to large segments of the citizenry, while some of the more traditional political concerns have become less significant as focal points for political interest and conflict. For a number of reasons these newer issues tend not to divide the population in the same way as did the more traditional concerns. Nor have stable coalitions of groups and interests formed around the newer issues in a way that can give meaningful shape and articulation to contemporary political life.

During the first half of this century, especially with the occurrence of the Great Depression and the advent of the New Deal, questions of providing for economic security and government regulation of economic and industrial life became the paramount political concerns. Partisan groupings and electoral coalitions formed basically around the questions of economic welfare and government regulation. For the most part the wealthy and the privileged tended to join together in opposing increased government intervention in social and economic relations. Those less well off tended to support government provisions for social and economic security and regulation. As a result of growing affluence, social and economic developments associated with advanced industrial society, or simply the formation of consensus over time, many of the traditional political issues pertaining to the role of government in economic and industrial relations have moved from center stage on the political agenda. They are less often the most salient and divisive foci of political interest and attention. This is not to say that the traditional economic and industrial issues are not of impor- tance to people, or that the problems associated with industrial society have been solved, or that there are not disagreements concerning economic and industrial relations issues. Rather, it seems that for many people these issues are relatively less salient, controversial, and crucial than they were in the past. Furthermore, a series of other issues and problems have become significant politically. They have become influential in shaping and structuring the political interests and choices of many people.

Among the important issues that have moved to center stage in the political agenda during the past decade are such things as U.S. involvement in Southeast Asia and maybe a more general concern with involvement of the U.S. in the world at large, race relations and particularly efforts to bring about integration and economic equality, the rise in crime and other forms of public and social disorder, concern for the environment, a generalized concern over national priorities, and questions concerning political trust and legitimacy. One of the leading issues in the area of social welfare of the 1970s—the proposition calling for some form of guaranteed minimum family income—is different both in its potential impact and its sources of support from the traditional issues of social welfare and economic security which were so important in focusing and structuring political relationships in previous decades. In the 1930s, 1940s, and early 1950s most of the industrial labor force and those less well off economically shared a common interest in pressing the rights of collective bargaining, unemployment compensation, retirement and old age benefits, and the like. A program that would provide for a minimum family income, by way of contrast, would benefit only the really poor—those without steady employment or adequate income. It would not be of direct interest or benefit to the majority of the industrial work force who have earned general job security and comparatively high levels of income. In addition to helping to pay for such a program through taxes while not receiving direct benefits from it, such a program can be construed as an ego threat to the industrial worker who has "worked his way up" to a position of job security and a decent income, and who has been socialized to believe that his labor is his major contribution to society and that one should be rewarded for the amount of work and productivity that he provides. As data to be presented later suggest, the skilled worker is particularly unenthusiastic about government income and living guarantees.

The growing concern and controversy over public order, which involve issues ranging from racial tensions to student demands and campus disorders, from industrial strife to crime in the streets, from drug usage, dress patterns, and sexual behavior to modes of political expression, have led in many instances to a questioning of governmental

intentions and important political values. These issues affect both
political authorities and the general population very differently from
the traditional issues of economic distribution and security. Along with
some aspects of the race issue and the controversies surrounding the
involvement in Southeast Asia, the issue of public order has given rise
to the disagreements and skepticism concerning the very operation of
American political institutions and procedures. Fundamental questions
are being asked about such basics as the role of Congress and the
presidency, the operation of the party system and electoral processes,
and the proper role of the courts and of law enforcement officials. Such
questioning and distrust have been accompanied by a substantial breach
between those who want rapid and extensive change and those who
seek even more tenaciously to preserve the status quo.

The sluggishness with which the government (or the system) has
responded to new interests and demands, the growth of discontent, and
the pressure for change are both a reflection of the confusion and
frustration noted above and factors that aggravate it. In a period
punctuated with considerable clamor for change—in some instances
changes wanted by large segments of the population—the political
response seems often to be stagnation and the skirting of issues, rather
than their resolution. The nonresponse, or at least the lack of decisive
response, can be seen in the national elections in 1968 and 1970. In the
midst of much commotion about change and "the new politics" in
1968, both the Republican and Democratic parties nominated
candidates who were tied in, at least symbolically, with the "old
politics," with ongoing policies, political procedures, and styles. The
leadership of both parties seemed unable or unwilling to respond very
effectively to, and in some instances even to cope with, the strong
concerns and vocal dissent being registered by much of the electorate.
McCarthy in the Democratic party, and to a much lesser extent
Rockefeller in the Republican party, became focal points for the call
for change and the expression of dissent. Neither of them was able to
win his party's nomination, nor to give effective long-run focus and
leadership to the many-faceted pressures for change. George Wallace,
working outside the confines of the major parties, was more effective in
articulating and responding to some of the pockets of the discontent
and frustration.

The fall 1968 campaign, rather than serving as a channel through which the controversy over Vietnam, racial integration, and other issues could be articulated and debated, proved more an exercise in skirting the issues. The Republican candidate avoided discussion of Vietnam almost entirely, pointing out that the incumbent president was in the midst of negotiations and that it would not be proper for him to espouse a clear policy position or to openly criticize policy. The Democratic candidate, on the other hand, because of the already open breach in his party over the Vietnam issue, could not completely avoid the question. His problem was to try to map out a position that would hold both prowar and antiwar elements together. This, of course, precluded a strong, clear position one way or the other. The presidential election and many of the congressional races, thus, were not forums in which the major issues of race and the war were clearly focused on, policies or courses of action clearly spelled out, or in which the voters were able to register their preferences or dissatisfactions concerning the issues that most concerned them. The close outcome of the election rendered the results all the more nondecisive.

The mushiness of issue articulation and lack of clear issue distinction between parties and candidates, one may wish to point out, is not unusual in American politics. It may well be the norm. However, the discrepancy between the concerns of the voters and the positions and concerns articulated by the parties and campaigns in 1968 seem to have been exceptionally great. The voters were more intensely concerned than usual about the activities or nonactivities of their government. Samuel Lubell pointed out how and why the lack of concrete issue focus was particularly troublesome in the context of the politics of 1968. In a chapter of *The Hidden Crisis in American Politics* entitled "The Revolt of the Voters," Lubell points out that with regard to the 1968 election the voters were particularly concerned about issues and wanted clear positions presented by the candidates. He comments: "Probably the most important single fact about the voters in 1968 was their intense emotional involvement in issues, an impatience that exceeded anything I have encountered in any previous presidential election." [5] The voters, he reports, were looking for candidates with clear issue stands with which they could identify on Vietnam, on race relations, and on other issues. Contrary to some interpretations of the content and outcome of the presidential race, which argue that Nixon won because he was skillfully able to avoid concrete policy commitments along with effective use of the image media, Lubell argues that the refusal of Nixon to focus clearly on those issues which were of concern to the voters cost him many votes. Commenting on this, Lubell says:

> My interviewing through the years has taught me that when people are only moderately concerned about something they will accept superficial generalities. But when their emotions and self-interests are deeply engaged, they demand meaningful detail and feel cheated if it is not given them.[6]

Many voters, he reports, were waiting for the candidates to offer clear, meaningful statements. They ended up feeling cheated. The congressional elections in 1968, as well as those in 1970, proved little more successful in addressing the major issues confronting the people or in suggesting what direction the people wished their government to take.

This is not the place to attempt to explain these electoral results or to analyze their meaning. It is hoped that the discussion that follows will shed some light on them. The reason for mentioning them here is to suggest some ways in which the political system is showing itself to be less than clear and decisive in reflecting and addressing some of the key problems and concerns of the citizenry. We are in a period marked with relatively high levels of concern and involvement over issues, over social, economic, and political problems. The "normal" channels of opinion mobilization, articulation, and representation, however, are finding it very difficult to respond to these concerns and to cope with dissatisfactions, frustrations, and pressures for change. This sluggishness of political response itself contributes in turn to the sense of frustration and confusion, as well as the disaffection from political institutions and processes.

SCOPE AND PLAN OF THE BOOK

The focus and subject matter of this discussion are limited. This book does not deal with all of the issues and concerns relevant to the study of public opinion or the impact of public opinion on the political system. It might be useful to spell out more clearly what the focus is and how the concerns will be developed.

There are some key areas of concern in the study of public opinion which will be entirely neglected, or approached only indirectly. The discussion does not deal with the individual and how and why he develops and holds various opinions. The subject of opinion and attitude formation and change among individuals (sometimes referred to as political socialization) has made up the bulk of the work falling under the rubric of public opinion. This factor reflects, in part, the strong influence that social psychology and sociology have had upon the development of public opinion studies. These processes are, of course, important for an understanding of public opinion, but they are not of direct concern to the more specific focus of this discussion.

Although we are concerned with the relationship between public opinion and public policy, how the opinions of the public affect the decisions of political leaders and the operation of the government, we approach that subject only indirectly. Like many other aspects of human affairs, it can be said that the relationship between public opinion and public policy is at the same time one of the most significant concerns and the most difficult to pin down. Relationships between opinions and policy are extremely complex and may follow a wide variety of patterns. We shall not attempt to assess the correspondence in regard to any particular issues or over any particular period of time. Nor will we attempt to ask whether any particular political decisions were or were not affected by public opinion. However, a careful spelling out of opinion distributions and how they are related to major institutions which link public opinion with policy makers, how political opinions are related to each other, and how the distributions of opinions are related to facets such as geographic location, social economic position, age, race, and the like will shed considerable light on both the impact of public opinion on governmental actions and the role of political leaders and public policy in shaping public opinion. More specifically, attention to these factors and changes in them over the past few decades should help us to understand the current political discontent and disarray.

This discussion is based primarily upon the analysis of the distributions of political opinions of American citizens over the past decade. Given the availability of public opinion data and the emphasis placed upon public opinion in American politics, it is surprising how few works have dealt systematically with patterns of opinion distributions.

V. O. Key's *Public Opinion and American Democracy,* published in 1961, remains one of the few efforts at an extensive probe of the distributions of political opinions and how these distributions affect the operation of American politics.[7] Although this effort is more modest in scope, theoretical focus, and length, the approach to the subject and many of the conceptual and theoretical concerns have been influenced greatly by that work by Key. Two differences should be noted. Key used the mid-1950s as his time base, employing data taken primarily from the 1956 Survey Research Center election study. This discussion focuses primarily on the period following the 1964 election through the early 1970s. In addition this analysis is more explicitly concerned with changes in opinion focus and distributions. It is an attempt both to identify opinion changes over the past decade and to discuss their consequences for American politics. More specifically the effort is to describe the political concerns and policy preferences of the American public, to analyze how political opinions are distributed and structured in the society, and to see how they relate to political parties and elections. By spelling out these factors we hope to gain a better understanding of the current political mood and of likely developments in American political life.

The discussion and analysis rest largely on the analysis of survey research or public opinion poll data. In the course of the discussion, data taken from different sources are presented and analyzed in several different forms. In order to assist the reader who may not be familiar with the nature and source of survey data or with some basic techniques of data presentation and analysis, we have included two appendixes following the basic text. Appendix A is a simple introductory statement on the nature of survey research. Appendix B offers a simple discussion of the basic modes of data presentation and analysis that are used in the book.

The core of the analysis presented is based on data taken from the 1968 University of Michigan Survey Research Center election survey. Data from the 1970 SRC election survey and from earlier SRC surveys are also used, as are data from Gallup Polls and surveys conducted by the Roper and the National Opinion Research Center survey organizations. Responses to a core set of questions, most of them taken from the 1968 SRC survey, are used in various forms throughout the book.

These questions deal with attitudes and preferences regarding contemporary political issues. The simple response frequencies for these items and the wording of the questions are presented in Chapter 2.

The plan of development for the book is as follows: In Chapter 2 we attempt to portray contemporary opinion distributions pertaining to a series of major issue areas, identifying areas of conflict and consensus, and patterns of stability and change over the past few years. In Chapter 3 we explore changes in issue focus and saliency and how different types of political opinions are related to each other. In Chapter 4 we turn to the question of how political opinions are structured by socioeconomic factors such as occupation and income and changes over the past several decades in the extent to which differences in opinion are related to differences in socioeconomic position. In Chapter 5 the concern is with the impact of several other factors—race, age, geographic region—in structuring political opinions. The question of whether or not persons with different levels of political involvement, participation, and efficacy tend to have different political interests and outlooks is explored in Chapter 6. In Chapter 7 opinion distributions are related to voting and political party preferences, and the consequences of such relations or nonrelations for the responsiveness of the political system are discussed. In the final chapter we attempt to bring these various threads together and to assess their bearing on both the contemporary period and the issue of public opinion and government in American society.

Notes

[1] The list of important political assassinations in the United States over the past decade includes President John Kennedy, Senator Robert Kennedy, Civil Rights leader Martin Luther King, Black Muslim leader Malcolm X, and American Nazi Party leader Lincoln Rockwell, as well as the attempted assassination of Alabama Governor George Wallace, Third Party presidential candidate in 1968 and candidate in the Democratic primaries in 1972.

[2] The trend in the South over the same time period has been toward an increase in turnout. The increased turnout in the South, however, reflects a different type of change. It reflects primarily the increase in voting among southern blacks as legal barriers to their voting have been removed. For this reason the southern states are not included in these particular figures.

[3] *Gallup Poll* (Fall 1971).

[4] *Gallup Political Index* (Princeton, N.J.: Gallup International No. 68 (February 1971), p. 34.

[5] Samuel Lubell, *The Hidden Crisis in American Politics* (New York: Norton, 1970), p. 47.

[6] Ibid., pp. 55–56.

[7] V. O. Key, Jr., *Public Opinion and American Democracy* (New York: Knopf, 1961).

CHAPTER 2
CONTEMPORARY
POLITICAL OPINIONS:
CONFLICT AND CONSENSUS

Over the past decade a wide variety of slogans and labels have been used to describe the political mood of the country and to catch the drift of popular opinion. In the mid-1960s the theme was consensus. Slogans such as the "politics of consensus," the "politics of implementation," and "reasoning together" were used by political leaders and commentators. Congress, following the Johnson landslide in 1964, enacted a number of new "liberal" domestic programs for which there was widespread popular support. Innovations in social and economic policy were adopted under conditions of general prosperity and, at least initially, without inciting strong intergroup hostilities.

Within only a few years, however, the tone had changed. The themes of "racial backlash," "a move to the right," "welfare state backlash," "neo-isolationism" were widely used. While in the mid-1960s the mood was characterized by consensus and working together to deal with problems, by the late 1960s and early 1970s crisis, conflict, and polarization had become the predominant themes. References to "crisis of authority," the "race crisis," the "environmental crisis," the "urban crisis," and the "crisis of national unity" became common. Some commentators have referred to a period of revolution; others to a movement toward repression. Nearly all regard the past decade as a period of change.

In this chapter we present a portrait of contemporary American political opinions. For what types of policies is there widespread support? For which, strong opposition and conflict? To what extent have there been changes in the past few years in popular opinion regarding social welfare programs, international involvement, race relations, and general support for the government? How does the citizenry feel about various contemporary government activities? What about proposed new programs and actions—price and wage controls, national health insurance, welfare reforms? Opinion data are presented to indicate simple distributions of opinions in a series of key issue areas: (1) domestic welfare and economic policies, (2) foreign affairs and international involvement, (3) U.S. involvement in Vietnam, (4) race relations and civil rights, (5) public order and crime, and (6) attitudes toward government. In addition to organizing the discussion of contemporary opinion distribution in this chapter, these issue area categories will be used to structure the discussion and analysis in the succeeding chapters.

One of the most significant issues in the consideration of public opinion is the extent of agreement or division within the population in regard to a proposition or series of issues. Patterns of conflict or consensus are particularly important in considering the political consequences of opinion distributions. Governments may choose to act or not to act in certain areas, depending on whether or not there is consensus or conflict concerning that area within the population. The stability of a given regime is dependent, in large part, on the level of consensus concerning its legitimacy and operating principles.

A consensus on a given issue exists within a population when a strong majority of the population holds the same opinion or preference and only a small minority holds an opposing viewpoint.[1] In the 1968 SRC election survey, respondents were asked whether they felt the U.S. should stay home and not concern itself with problems in other parts of the world. Twenty-four percent of those responding agreed with the proposition that we would be better off if we stayed home. Seventy-six percent disagreed with the proposition. These responses indicate a consensus in support of U.S. concern with world problems. Such a distribution of opinions can be diagramed as shown in Figure 2.1.

A question posed in the same SRC 1968 survey, asking whether or not the respondent favored the government in Washington seeing that white and black children are allowed to go to the same schools, elicited a different pattern of responses. Of those responding, 43 percent felt that the government should see to it; 50 percent said that it should not.

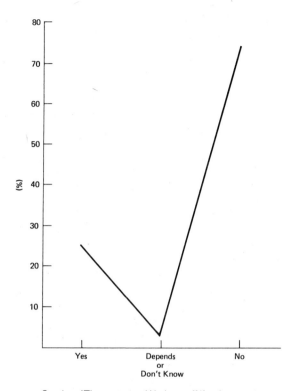

Question: "The country would be better off if we just stayed home and did not concern ourselves with problems in other parts of the world."

Data from the 1968 SRC election survey.

FIGURE 2.1   Distribution of opinions showing consensus

These responses constitute a conflict situation. Half of the respondents oppose federal intervention. Slightly less than half are in favor. This conflict distribution when diagramed forms a different curve, as in Figure 2.2.

The past decade has been characterized at different points as a period of consensus and of great conflict. During the early years of his administration President Johnson talked a good deal about the prevalent feeling of consensus. By the 1968 election most commentators were noting the high level of conflict that had developed. We are now in a period of conflict, conflicts over new types of issues and

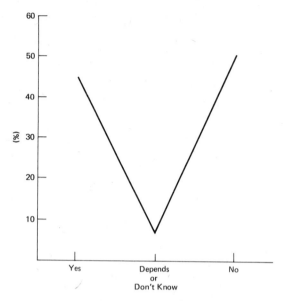

Question: "Do you think the government in Washington should see to it that White and Negro children go to the same schools?"

Data from the 1968 SRC election survey.

FIGURE 2.2 Distribution of opinions—conflict

structured by patterns different from those of the immediate past. We appear in the midst of a period of change—important change in which traditional patterns of conflict are passing away, and new ones have not yet formed.

In this chapter we describe the patterns of conflict and consensus with respect to both the newer and the more traditional political issues. Before moving on to explore contemporary opinion distributions, however, let us discuss an approach to recent American political development which is particularly relevant to an attempt to understand some of the changes in the patterns of consensus and cleavage which we have alluded to. This interpretation has to do with the impact of affluence upon American political life, or the political consequences of advanced industrialization. A brief discussion of some of these notions may help to place the subsequent description and analysis in a larger perspective.

The question of how American life and politics have been influenced by wealth and bountiful resources is not a new one. Alexis de Tocqueville, writing about America in the 1840s, commented on the tendency of European analysts to stress the abundance of resources in their interpretations of American society.[2] However, economic and technological developments in the last two decades have led to new and somewhat different emphases. Recent social commentators have argued that the United States and, to a somewhat lesser degree, other advanced industrial societies have entered a new era, an age of economic abundance or affluence. They point to the existence of a vast productive capacity which creates economic, social, and political conditions that are qualitatively different from any that preceded them. Galbraith's book *The Affluent Society*, published in 1958, had much to do both with popularizing the theme of affluence and setting out some of the basic dimensions and issues relative to the affluent society.[3]

One explicit statement of ideas concerning the impact of affluence on American political life was presented by Robert E. Lane in a 1965 article entitled "The Politics of Consensus in an Age of Affluence."[4] In that article Lane asserted the existence of affluence, outlined its basic characteristics, spelled out a series of assumptions and hypotheses about its impact on American politics, and investigated some of these relationships with public opinion data. Lane's major notions and basic argument will be presented here in some detail because they represent an important line of thought concerning political life in modern society and because they are addressed directly to the present period and to the issues of opinion conflict and consensus with which we are concerned. Lane's basic argument seems closely related to some of the assumptions underlying President Johnson's Great Society. The article was published during the high point of Great Society efforts and support, at a time when Johnson was stressing both the high level of consensus and the great potential for political and social advancement that flowed from conditions of affluence and economic growth.

Lane argues that the United States entered what he terms the "age of affluence" sometime in the 1950s. This concept as he used it entails a combination of economic conditions and governmental policies that include (1) a relatively high level of per capita income, (2) a distribution of income that is relatively equalitarian, (3) a good rate of growth in Gross National Product per capita, (4) provisions against the hazards of life through programs such as social security, unemployment benefits, and the like, and (5) a managed economy which involves the use of fiscal and monetary powers to smooth out the business cycle and provide for economic growth.[5] Positing the existence of the "age of affluence," Lane poses the question of how the development of such affluence relates to political behavior and attitudes in the contemporary period. In hypothesizing about the political consequences of affluence, he foresees a set of conditions which he labels the "politics of consensus." Affluence, he contends, leads to the lessening of hostility between parties and religious groups and to a *rapprochement* between men and their government. Hostile cleavages, he suggests, lose their emotional and political impact. The shape of political cleavages is altered from a situation in which the public is more or less evenly divided to conflicts in which the division is between a main body of opinion and a small and dwindling minority. The major body of opinion, he seems to imply, would be supportive of the policies and programs that make up the modern welfare state and promote affluence.

Lane develops six major themes as components of this consensus. They merit direct quotation here. He hypothesizes that "In the Age of Affluence [11] :

    (a) people will come increasingly to trust each other, to feel less at the mercy of chance and more in control of their lives, and so to be more optimistic regarding the future. These changes in turn will promote others;

    (b) people will slowly lose their sense of high national, personal, and group stakes in elections; political partisanship, while not changing on the surface, will change its meaning;

    (c) people will slowly change their class awareness and consciousness, so that the relationship between ideology and class status will change; but occupation and class will continue to influence electoral choice—even as the electoral "pivot" shifts;

    (d) religious institutions and dogmas will slowly lose their influence over men's secular thought, inter-faith hostility will decline, but religious community identification may retain a constant political "cuing" function;

    (e) the struggle for racial equality will be facilitated by affluence and its associated attitudes, but the sense of crisis and strife in this arena will continue or grow for an indefinite period;

(f)   there will be a rapproachement between men and their government and a decline of political alienation.[6]

Lane presents a scattering of public opinion trend data that offer
some support for the hypothesized changes in the outlook of the public
from the 1930s to the early 1960s. The data presented appear to
support his basic thesis. The article, it should be kept in mind, was
published at the high point of the era of consensus that existed for a
brief period following the 1964 election and prior to the serious
escalation of the Vietnam conflict. The existence of a broad-based
consensus, the waning of antiwelfare state animosity, and the dampening of industrial strife were very much the topics of the day.

Needless to say, developments in the past few years cast doubt on
Lane's thesis. The discussion in the preceding chapter suggests that the
term "politics of consensus" is not an apt label for contemporary
American political life. The past few years have been marked by sharp,
often bitter and bewildering conflicts. It seems particularly apparent
that the growing *rapprochement* between man and government and the
decrease in social and political alienation which Lane projected have
not occurred. The evidence, both impressionistic and from opinion
survey data, point to decreases in personal and political trust and
optimism since the mid-1960s. There is much in what has occurred to
suggest the rejection of Lane's thesis that economic affluence would be
followed by a politics of consensus, especially as he outlined such
consensus.

Before rejecting the line of reasoning proposed by Lane, however, it
is useful to look more closely at some basic underlying assumptions.
Lane's argument seems to rest on several notions about the relationship
between economics and politics in industrial society. His argument
seems to assume that political preferences and political conflict stem,
rather exclusively, from economic and class-oriented interests. Political
outlooks and interests center primarily around problems of economic
distribution and security. This approach is accepted by many theorists
who focus on the relationship between class and politics. Lane's
argument contends further that affluence, accompanied by the
economic and social policies of the welfare state, dampens the
importance and intensity of economic, industrial, and class-oriented
conflicts. Affluence seems to permit relatively high incomes, job
security, and provisions for adversity for the industrial worker. At the

same time governmental policies do not constitute a threat to the
position and well-being of the privileged. Government, through a series
of policies and programs that regulate the economy, works to assure
prosperity and economic growth. The growth and affluence, in turn,
contribute to the material well-being of all, or at least most. Under
these conditions the forces creating intense antagonism between
economic and class groupings are muffled. By the same token the stakes
that various economic, religious, and partisan groups have in the
outcome of electoral and other political decisions are rendered less
crucial.

Given this interpretation of politics and of the impact of affluence
on social and economic antagonisms, the predicted outcome is a
far-reaching political consensus. The basis of political controversy and
of political alienation, Lane seems to imply, is class conflict centering
around the distribution of wealth and industrial relations. The politics
of consensus comes about as the scarcity and economic insecurity
which give rise to politically relevant and intense economic conflicts are
diminished.

Lane may be correct in his assumptions about the impact of
affluence and advanced industrialization on economic and class
conflicts. That thesis fits in with some of the changes in the structuring
of political opinions, the shift in issue focus, and the contemporary
disarray that are the central themes in this discussion. However, the
argument that the development of great affluence and the dampening
of class and group antagonisms lead to consensus politics, higher levels
of interpersonal trust, and a *rapprochement* between man and his
government does not hold. It appears that new forms of conflicts,
conflicts that do not follow so closely the traditional lines of economic
and class antagonisms, can develop in the wake of affluence and
advanced industrialization. Political antagonisms and cleavages that very
deeply divide the citizenry may develop outside the framework of the
conventional economic and class lines of industrial society. These
notions will be developed more fully in later chapters.

We turn now to look at the patterns of conflict and of consensus in
contemporary American society. If there has been a move from
widespread consensus in the mid-1960s to considerable conflict in the
late sixties and early seventies, in what areas have the changes taken

place? Has there been a move to the right? Has there occurred a strong
reaction against the welfare state? Has there been a backlash in the area
of civil rights?

DOMESTIC WELFARE AND ECONOMIC POLICIES

During most of the twentieth century domestic welfare and economic
issues have been the primary concerns of government and most of the
citizenry. They have been the focal point for legislative and policy-
making bodies, as well as the bases of partisan and electoral struggles.
Over the past four decades government, especially the federal government, has moved toward an extensive involvement in the economic,
social, and industrial life of American society. This movement has
included regulation of business, industry, and labor; provisions for
social and economic security; monetary and fiscal policies designed to
promote economic growth and to avoid recessions and inflation; and a
series of programs designed to assist in providing for housing, urban
redevelopment, education, highway construction, and agriculture
support. During the 1930s, when much of this increased involvement
was initiated, and also through the 1940s and 1950s, the general
proposition of government involvement, as well as many specific
activities, were widely disputed. There was considerable conflict over
these welfare state measures. Democrats, organized labor, and those less
well off economically tended to support them. Republicans, business
associations, and the more privileged tended to oppose them.

Until 1965 there was sufficient opposition to block congressional
enactment of programs such as substantial federal aid to education and
medical assistance for the elderly. Following the Goldwater defeat in
the 1964 election, programs in these and other areas were enacted.
Some of these measures had been debated in Congress for nearly three
decades without enactment. The mid-1960s also saw the enactment of
other welfare and economic measures designed to combat poverty and
to assist cities and states in dealing with urban problems. The 1964
election has been interpreted by some as a watershed election in the
development of the role of government in the society. It has been
viewed as a significant and solid defeat for those opposed to the basic
programs and commitments of the welfare state.

By 1964 there was a good majority of opinion in support of standard welfare state measures. The distributions of opinions approximated Lane's description of political consensus in the "Age of Affluence;" that is, a division made up of a strong majority in support and a small and dwindling minority in opposition. A substantial amount of public opinion data document the existence of widespread support for both general and particular welfare state measures by the mid-1960s. In their presidential election studies from 1956 through 1968 the University of Michigan Survey Research Center asked a set of questions pertaining to support for several general areas of domestic activity by the federal government: federal aid to education, low cost hospital and medical assistance, and job guarantees. As far back as 1956 there were strong margins of support for federal government activity in each of these areas.[7] The percentages of persons in a series of surveys responding favorably to the proposition that the government in

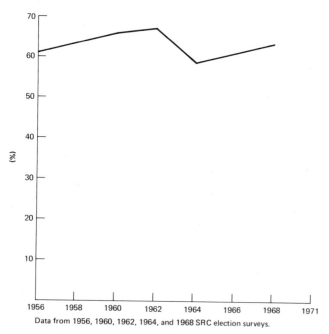

Data from 1956, 1960, 1962, 1964, and 1968 SRC election surveys.

FIGURE 2.3 Percent favoring medical assistance proposition, 1956–1968

Washington should help see to it that people could get hospital and medical care at low cost are shown in graph form in Figure 2.3.

The data suggest fairly stable and high levels of support for government medical assistance, with margins running approximately 2 to 1 in favor at each of the five data points. The questions dealing with federal aid to education and job guarantees also received high margins of support from 1956 through 1962. In the 1964 and 1968 surveys the wording of the questions was altered in such a way as to make the items noncomparable.

The same high levels of support were evident for more specific welfare and economic policies and programs. A survey conducted by the Gallup organization and reported on in *The Political Beliefs of Americans* asked respondents their opinions on several particular programs and policy goals that were of concern at the time.[8] The responses to six such items are presented in Table 2.1. They show levels of support ranging from two-thirds to three-fourths for each of the programs. Free and Cantril used the responses to these six issue items to develop an "operational spectrum" index, one dimension of a liberal-conservative stance. They found that 65 percent of the respondents fell in either the "completely liberal" or "predominately liberal" categories.[9] That is, about two-thirds of the respondents disagreed with none or only one of the six programs or propositions, a general consensus in support of welfare state activities.

TABLE 2.1 Level of support for several economic welfare type programs or goals, 1964

Reduce Unemployment (Percent agree)	78%
Do Away with Poverty (Percent agree)	75%
Federal Aid to Education (Percent for)	67%
Federal Housing Program (Support at present level or more)	72%
Federal Urban Renewal (Support at present level or more)	74%
Compulsory Medical Insurance for Elderly (Percent approve)	66%

Source: Data from Public Opinion Surveys Study No. 637 (October, 1964).

More recent opinion data regarding several welfare policies suggest that the level of support for certain types of welfare programs has remained rather stable. In a December 1968 Gallup Poll 64 percent of the respondents reported favoring the equalization of welfare payments among the states, a notion that became a part of President Nixon's welfare reform package. [10] In a May 1969 Gallup survey 60 percent of the respondents answered affirmatively when asked, "Would you favor or oppose giving food stamps at a greatly reduced rate to families whose earnings are $20.00 to $60.00 a week?" [11] In July of that year respondents were asked how they felt about the federal government providing funds to set up community day-care centers so that mothers living in poor areas could take jobs and so that children could get early educational training. Sixty-four percent reported that they favored such a program; 30 percent opposed it. [12]

In regard to two newer welfare type issues, however, opinion distributions are different. Currently, two of the most important and controversial proposed developments in government welfare and security provisions are the proposals calling for some sort of guaranteed minimum family income and a comprehensive national health insurance program. The first was included as one of the measures in President Nixon's 1969 welfare reform package. The health insurance proposal is at an initial stage of formulation as a serious political issue. It is, however, almost certain to be a major question for public debate and congressional consideration in the next few years.

Despite the endorsement of many prominent economists, welfare experts, and even the Republican administration, there has been little popular support for the concept of a guaranteed minimum family income. In a January 1969 survey Gallup asked: "As you know, there is talk about giving every family an income of at least $3200.00 a year, which would be the amount for a family of four. If the family earns less than this, the government would make up the difference. Would you favor or oppose such a plan?" [13] Less than a third (32 percent) reported favoring this proposal, 62 percent opposed it, and 6 percent had no opinion. These responses are similar to those obtained in the SRC 1964 and 1968 election surveys when the notion of guaranteeing a good standard of living was combined with the job guarantee item. Approximately a third of the respondents in 1964 and 1968 reported agreement with the notion that "the government in Washington should see to it that every person has a job and a good standard of living." The people seem to make a distinction between guaranteeing an income or standard of living, on the one hand, and guaranteeing job opportunities, on the other hand. This distinction becomes even more evident from responses to a different proposal asked in the same January 1969 survey as the income guarantee item discussed above. The question posed was: "Another proposal is to guarantee enough work so that each family that has an employable wage earner be guaranteed enough work each week to give him a wage of about $60.00 a week or $3,200.00 a year. Would you favor or oppose such a plan?" [14] For this item the responses were Favor, 79 percent; Oppose, 16 percent; and No Opinion, 5 percent. It would seem that the factor that people oppose in the minimum family income proposal is not the proposition of government involvement but, rather, the proposal that people be provided an income without having to work for it.

An item in the 1970 SRC survey found the electorate divided on the issue of government health insurance. The question asked the respondent to place himself on a seven-point scale with a government health insurance plan at one end and private insurance at the other. Of the respondents answering the item 45 percent placed themselves on the government insurance side; 40 percent chose positions on the private insurance side; 15 percent chose the point falling in the middle. Although those favoring some sort of government insurance had a slight margin, the data suggest that there is no consensus on one side or the other. The proposal for a government health program at this point lacks the widespread support evident for many welfare measures, including the Medicare program for the aged. On the other hand, it does not evoke the strong opposition among the public that the guaranteed family income proposition does.

The period of economic inflation which followed the escalation of involvement in Vietnam led to considerable interest in price and wage controls. A series of polls taken between February 1966 and October 1970 by Gallup found the population fairly evenly divided in response to the question: "It has been suggested that price and wages (salaries) be 'frozen'—that is, kept at their present level as long as the war in Vietnam lasts. Do you think this is a good idea or a poor idea?" [15] In all but one of five polls there was a slight margin of support for the proposition, but never by more than a few percentage points. After resisting pressures for controls for two years, President Nixon, in August of 1971, issued a 90-day freeze on prices and wages and at the end of the 90-day freeze a system of wage and price controls was put into effect. As is often the case, once the policy had been enacted popular opinion lined up very strongly behind price and wage controls. A question asked by Gallup in October 1971, toward the end of the 90-day freeze but prior to the announcement concerning the second phase of controls, found that 35 percent of the respondents wanted to keep price-wage controls as they were under the 90-day freeze and 51 percent wanted to keep price-wage controls but change the way they were applied. Only 12 percent wanted to give up all price-wage controls. [16] These responses indicate an extremely strong level of support for this new instance of economic regulation. Whether price and wage controls will be a short-term proposition or a permanent change in economic relationships remains to be seen.

Additional examples of opinion distributions regarding domestic economic, welfare, and industrial relations policies could be presented. However, the major dimensions of opinions in this policy area should be clear. There has existed, at least over the past decade, a strong majority in support of a wide range of programs that fall under the rubric "welfare state." Although there is concern expressed over the cost of some welfare programs and there is disagreement over the administration of some welfare state measures, there is little to indicate that the general consensus in support of basic welfare state commitments is diminishing. Politicians may seek votes by pledging to get rid of welfare "chiselers" and by threatening to throw HEW personnel into the Potomac. The rhetoric, however, does not indicate popular support for moving away from the complex of structures providing for economic security and economic and industrial regulation that have been developed over the past four decades. If there has been a move to the right or toward a more conservative climate as some have contended, it has not been directed toward the dismantling of basic welfare state provisions. Moreover, as shall be made clearer in the next chapter, economic security and industrial relations issues seem to have become less salient politically to large portions of the public over the past decade or so.

There are areas of conflict and even widespread opposition over some types of welfare provisions as well as growing frustrations over the rising costs of other types of welfare programs. For the most part there is considerable hostility to programs involving income transfers and special consideration for the really poor. Because a good portion of those categorized at the poverty level or below—especially those who are most visible—are blacks, feelings regarding these types of welfare provisions have become closely intertwined with racial feelings. This seems to be the case with family-income maintenance proposals. As we pointed out above, there is considerable opposition to the idea of providing every family with a basic minimum income. Some components of the series of anti-poverty programs that were enacted during the mid-1960s have engendered similar opposition over the past few years.

The issue of a national health insurance program would seem to represent a different situation. Although opinion seems to be rather closely divided over the issue now, we would guess that as the issue becomes more clearly and forcefully articulated opinions regarding it will more closely approximate the more general consensus over economic welfare issues than those regarding issues such as the minimum family-income maintenance idea. We would guess that proposals for a national health insurance program will be more clearly formulated, that a consensus in support will be developed, and a program put into effect in the near future. It is doubtful that there will be the protracted discussion and delay that occurred in regard to the Medicare program during the late 1950s and early 1960s.

FOREIGN AFFAIRS AND INTERNATIONAL INVOLVEMENT

A second major issue area is that of foreign affairs or international involvement. Over the past few decades foreign policy concerns have come to take an increasingly greater proportion of time and attention of policy makers at the federal level. They have from time to time become primary issues in national elections. The Korean conflict had an impact upon the 1952 presidential election, and the Vietnam conflict affected the conduct and outcome of elections in 1968 and 1972.

One of the most important political developments of the post-World War II era has been the assumption by the United States of an active involvement in world affairs and the acceptance of this by large segments of the public. During much of its early history the United

States was not closely involved in international affairs. Even following its participation in World War I, the United States returned to a stance of noninvolvement. During the 1920s and 1930s isolationism, neutrality, and even pacifism were popular and influential political movements. Since World War II, however, the United States has played an active role in world affairs and has assumed a wide range of foreign commitments. This involvement has included participation in international organizations and a number of treaty agreements. It has entailed varied programs of military and economic aid. It has also included a number of military incursions and two controversial wars.

In general the growth of international involvement has been followed by public acceptance of this participation. Over the past twenty-five years there has been an increasing acceptance of the proposition that the U.S. should be concerned with world affairs. In most of its election studies from 1948 through 1968 the SRC asked whether the U.S. had gone too far in being concerned with the problems in other parts of the world. Although the questions asked in the 1948, 1952, and 1954 surveys are not quite the same as those asked in the later surveys, they can be viewed together to suggest the pattern of support. The responses to these items are presented in Figure 2.4. In 1948 and 1954 somewhat over half of the respondents rejected the proposition that the country had gone too far in concerning itself with problems in other parts of the world. In 1952, however, only 26 percent answered the same item negatively. The year 1952 is the only time point at which a majority disapproved of the extent of international involvement. Those responses undoubtedly represent the negative feelings many people had concerning involvement in Korea, an important issue in 1952.

From 1956 through 1968 respondents showed consistent and growing opposition to the proposition that the country would be better off if we stayed home. From 1956 to 1968 the proportion rejecting the isolationist stand increased 10 percentage points. It is interesting to note that in 1968, when there was considerable anguish concerning involvement in Vietnam, rejection of the stay-at-home proposition was at its highest. Differences in wording prohibit an accurate comparison of the 1968 responses with the 1952 opinions. It seems, however, that the public was less ready to reject the proposition of international involvement during the Vietnam war than during the Korean war. The data indicate the existence of a rather strong and steady consensus in

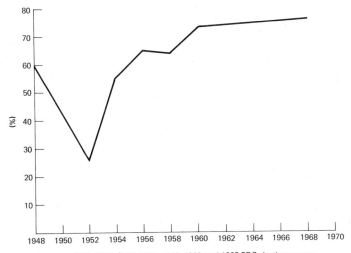

Data from 1948, 1952, 1954, 1956, 1958, 1960, and 1968 SRC election surveys.

FIGURE 2.4. Percent opposing U.S. isolation, 1948–1968

support of the involvement of the U.S. in world affairs.

Foreign economic aid has not enjoyed a margin of support as high as the general notion of involvement. Although foreign aid has been an important component of American foreign policy since the end of World War II and has been more or less strongly endorsed by both Republican and Democratic presidents, there have remained large pockets of opposition and apathy with respect to it. The data in Table 2.2 show the distribution of opinions in response to a series of

TABLE 2.2 Attitude toward foreign aid, 1956–1968

Responses	1956[a]	1960[a]	1964[b]	1968[b]
Yes	51% (756)	60% (1002)	59% (819)	46% (622)
Depends	18% (268)	17% (281)	20% (285)	22% (298)
No	31% (449)	24% (401)	21% (291)	32% (436)

Source: Data from SRC surveys, 1956, 1960, 1964, 1968.

[a] The wording of the question in 1956 and 1960 was: "The United States should give economic help to poorer countries of the world even if they can't pay for it."

[b] The wording for the question in 1964 and 1968 was: "Some say that we should give aid to other countries if they need help, while others think that each country should make its own way as best it can." "Have you been interested enough in this to favor one side over the other? (IF YES) Which opinion is most like yours?"

questions asking opinions on foreign aid from 1956 through 1968. Support for the aid proposition reached a high point of 60 percent in 1960. The lowest level of support is indicated in the 1968 survey, the only time in which support fell below 50 percent. Note that a relatively high proportion of respondents chose a position that lies between "Yes" and "No" in each year. Approximately one in five respondents fell in the "Depends" category. Although there consistently have been somewhat more respondents favoring than opposing foreign aid, there has been less than a strong consensus behind foreign economic aid. The 13 percentage point drop in the level of support for aid between 1964 and 1968 suggests that the trend may be toward less rather than more support. This coincides with the decrease in the size of foreign aid appropriations enacted over the past few years and the temporary refusal of the Senate in the fall of 1971 even to pass the foreign aid authorization.

Another major component of American foreign policy in the post–World War II era has been the development and maintenance of a strong military force. Very large military appropriations, military conscription, and the development and deploying of major defense systems have been a major condition of our economic and political life during the past few decades. During most of this period expenditures for defense have been passed without much opposition, either in Congress or among the general public. In the past few years, however, there has been an increased tendency to question defense appropriations. Congress has come to give closer scrutiny to defense appropriations and in some cases to vote against certain types of requested expenditures. Considerable opposition to the size of military expenditures has also developed among the public. Gallup polls taken in December 1968, July 1969, and May 1971 found that approximately half of the respondents reported either feeling that defense expenditures should be decreased (53 percent in 1968), or that too much money was being spent for defense (52 percent in 1969 and 49 percent in 1971).[17] Very few reported thinking that too little was being spent for defense. In both the 1969 and 1971 surveys 31 percent thought that present levels of spending were about right.

These figures document what debate in Congress and public discussion have indicated—a new area of conflict. In an area that had been beyond the pale of public question or controversy there has developed widespread public dissatisfaction and in many instances strong and organized opposition. This development took place during involvement in a military conflict, albeit an unpopular one. The movement toward dissatisfaction with defense spending is related to other contemporary factors. It is closely tied in with the deep sense of frustration and disillusionment over the military involvement in Southeast Asia. It is also tied in with the general concern for a reordering of national priorities.

Public reaction toward international involvement is confusing as we enter the decade of the 1970s. It is likely to become more so. There has been and may well continue to be a strong consensus in support of the proposition that the United States should be involved in the affairs of the world. There is likely to be increasing disagreement, however, as to the form and extent that involvement should take. Support for foreign economic assistance may continue to dwindle. Gigantic expenditures for the military are likely to remain controversial. Opposition to future military incursions is likely to be strong. The position of the United States in relationship to other nations—politically, economically, and militarily—is in the midst of fundamental shifts. At the end of World War II the United States stood as the dominant world power, politically, militarily, and, above all, economically. It held that position for some time. Over the past decade or so the growth in military and political strength of first the Soviet Union and more recently China, the recovery of Europe, and the economic growth of Japan and Germany have come to restrict that domination severely. These alterations, especially as they become intertwined with internal factors, are producing new tensions and areas of conflict. These tensions and conflicts have been, of course, most apparent in public reactions regarding the Vietnam conflict.

VIETNAM

The most significant political issue of the past decade has been the question of U.S. military involvement in Vietnam, or what might be more accurately labeled Southeast Asia. Although this is a foreign policy issue concerned with U.S. involvement in world affairs we consider it separately here. First, it is by itself significant enough to merit special consideration in any discussion of patterns of conflict and consensus in contemporary American politics. Second, as will be made clearer in the next chapter, opinion distributions on Vietnam have tended to be independent and unrelated to other types of general foreign affairs opinions. In addition, the controversy over Vietnam has precipitated other areas of questioning and conflict. These issues range from the scope of legitimate political dissent to the role of Congress in the making of foreign policy and the conduct of war, from the use of military conscription to citizen participation in candidate selection, and from the role of the United States in world affairs to the role of the military in American society.

The Vietnam conflict was the longest war in which the United States became involved. It has also been one of the most controversial. The demonstrations and marches, the disruptions at colleges and universities and at the 1968 Democratic convention, the various conspiracy trials, the shootings at Kent State University, the auto bumper stickers which read, "America, Love It or Leave It"—all bear witness to the scope of conflict and intensity of feelings generated by the Vietnam conflict. Here we wish to look at some of the basic dimensions and trends in public opinion regarding the Vietnam involvement as they were tapped by a number of surveys. Public support and opposition to the Vietnam conflict are probably among the most extensively measured sets of political attitudes in our history. Almost every month Gallup asked questions concerning some aspect of the involvement. Questions pertaining to Vietnam were posed in 1964, 1966, 1968, and 1970 SRC studies. This wealth of data allows one to look at variations of public opinion over a short, but important span of time. A wide range of public opinion questions have been asked about Vietnam, including responses to particular actions or policies. We shall consider two major aspects—ones that have been tapped periodically and that seem basic for the assessment of the extent and shape of conflict or consensus. These are the questions concerning whether or not the respondent thought that the involvement was a mistake and what course of action the respondent would like to see pursued in the future.

From that point at which there was first serious talk about extensive military involvement in Vietnam in 1964 and the public announcement in 1965 of the decision to send in large numbers of troops, through 1971 there occurred a complete reversal in public evaluation of whether or not U.S. involvement had been a mistake. The Survey Research Center asked the following question in 1964, 1968, and again in 1970: "Do you think we did the right thing in getting into the fighting in Vietnam, or should we have stayed out?" The trend in responses to this question is presented in Table 2.3. The data show that in 1964, 60 percent of the respondents answering the item thought that we did the right thing. By 1968 only 36 percent took the same position, while 62 percent thought we should have stayed out. The division of opinion in 1970 was much the same as in 1968. In only a few years public opinion moved from a position of fairly strong support for the correctness of initial involvement to one of strong opposition. The data further indicate that the reversal had occurred by the time of the 1968 election.

Gallup used a similar question, posing it more frequently than the SRC. From 1965 to the end of the war, the following question was asked periodically: "In view of the developments since we entered the fighting in Vietnam, do you think the U.S. made a mistake sending troops to fight in Vietnam?" Responses to this item ranging from August 1965 to the fall of 1971 are graphed in Figure 2.5. To the extent available data make it possible, the data points used represent roughly six-month intervals. The graph shows a pattern very similar to that found in the SRC surveys. The availability of more data points, however, allows the reader to see not only the overall change, but also the amount of change that occurred between various time points. Like the SRC data, the Gallup polls indicate that the change from strong support to strong opposition took place prior to the 1968 election. Significant jumps in the proportion of persons saying that we made a mistake occurred between the spring and fall of 1966 and again

TABLE 2.3 Right to get involved in Vietnam: 1964, 1968, and 1970

Right to get involved?[a]	1964	1968	1970
Yes, we did the right thing	60%	36%	38%
Depends (other)	2	2	
No, we should have stayed out	39	62	62

Source: Data from SRC surveys, 1964, 1968, 1970.

[a] Wording of question: "Do you think we did the right thing in getting into the fighting in Vietnam or should we have stayed out?"

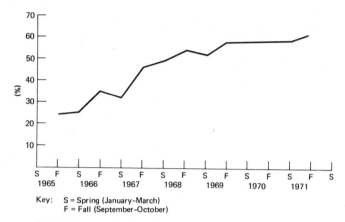

Key: S = Spring (January–March)
      F = Fall (September–October)

Wording of question: "In view of the developments since we entered the fighting in Vietnam, do you think the U.S. made a mistake sending troops to fight in Vietnam?"

Data from Gallup Opinion Index (1965 through 1971).

FIGURE 2.5.   Percent of the opinion that Vietnam was a mistake, 1965–1971

between the spring and fall of 1967. By the spring of 1968 more respondents thought the involvement a mistake than otherwise. From 1969 through 1971 the rate of change slowed down, though the movement was in the same direction.

The measure of whether or not people thought the involvement was a mistake may indicate overall evaluation of the war and the success of U.S. efforts in it. It is not, however, a particularly accurate indicator of what direction one would like the war effort to have taken. By 1968 and 1969 both those who thought it was wrong for the U.S. to have intervened for moral reasons and those who were unhappy because the war had not been quickly and devastatingly won may have been prepared to say that entrance into the conflict was a mistake. Much of the controversy concerned the alternatives of escalation versus de-escalation, between staying in and getting out. In its 1964, 1968, and 1970 surveys the Survey Research Center asked a question that tried to assess what type of future action the respondent would prefer. The question was: "Which of the following do you think we should do now in Vietnam?" The three alternative responses provided were "(1) Pull out of Vietnam entirely, (2) Keep our soldiers in Vietnam but try to end the fighting, or (3) Take a stronger stand even if it means invading North Vietnam." The relative choice of frequencies for these alternatives in each of the three surveys is presented in Table 2.4.

The trend data in Table 2.4 indicate, again, a significant shift in opinion. The shift was away from "take a stronger stand" and toward "pull out entirely." The percentage of those supporting the "pull out" alternative nearly tripled between 1964 and 1970. Those supporting a strong stand decreased from almost half to slightly more than a quarter. Unlike the trend with respect to the item asking whether the involvement had been a mistake, the change occurs both between 1964 and 1968 and between 1968 and 1970. The same trend is apparent in the responses to the Vietnam action scale ratings which are shown in Table 2.4.

At no point do the data on proposed courses of action suggest a consensus on policy alternatives. In both 1968 and 1970 opinion was very much divided with no alternative coming close to even a simple

TABLE 2.4 Opinions on what should be done in Vietnam, 1964, 1968, and 1970

What to do now in Vietnam?[a]	1964	1968	1970
Pull out of Vietnam entirely	14%	21%	38%
Keep our soldiers in Vietnam but try to end the fighting	38	39	36
Take a stronger stand even if it means invading North Vietnam	49	36	26
Other		4	

Position on Vietnam action scale[b]	1964	1968	1970
1. Immediate withdrawal	[c]	15%	24%
2.		9	8
3.		8	11
4.		30	24
5.		10	9
6.		9	6
7. Complete military victory		19	19

Source: Data from SRC surveys, 1964, 1968, 1970.

[a] Wording of question: "Which of the following do you think we should now do in Vietnam?"

[b] This item called for the respondent to rate himself on a Vietnam action scale. The extremes are "immediate withdrawal" at one end and "complete military victory" on the other end. The respondent was to place himself in one of seven positions.

[c] Item not used in 1964.

majority. [18] Gallup Poll data from 1971 and 1972 indicated growing support for setting a deadline for withdrawal and for withdrawing at a more rapid rate. The cease-fire agreed to in early 1973 may or may not bring an end to active military intervention in Southeast Asia. It is not likely, however, to resolve the many political, military, and moral conflicts which that involvement has engendered. The military involvement in Vietnam has created a number of divisions in American society that are likely to remain as part of American politics for considerable time.

CIVIL RIGHTS AND RACE RELATIONS

The issue of race relations also has emerged over the past decade or so as a major area of social and political conflict. Starting with the Supreme Court rulings, civil rights legislation passed by Congress, presidential statements and orders, laws passed by cities and states, the actions of numerous civil rights and other groups, concern about relations between blacks and whites, and the place of the blacks and other minorities in white-dominated society have increased both in scope and intensity. After nearly two decades of debate, confrontation, pressure, and governmental action there has been no subsiding of the passions and conflicts that surround the question of race relations. Racial conflicts, tensions between blacks and whites, and agitation over race or civil rights policies have been related to many of the disruptions and politically motivated acts of violence that have taken place over the past decade.

The question of relationships between racial groupings is a multi-faceted set of concerns. It includes desegregation of the schools and places of public accommodation, voting and political rights, equality in employment and economic provisions, access to housing or residential segregation, and the more amorphous question of black power, black culture, and black identity. Despite the concern expressed by political leaders and the intervention of government at nearly all levels there is considerable skepticism about how much change has occurred in race relations and in the condition of life for nonwhites. There is much talk of increasing racial polarization. Race relations remain a crucial American dilemma, a focal point of political conflict and cleavage. Race relates to political conflict in two ways. First, there are conflicts over policies and conditions having to do with the rights or well-being of blacks and with relationships between the races. This is the focus of discussion here. Second, there is the role of racial groupings in structuring political conflict. Do whites and nonwhites tend to have different political interests and values in program areas other than race? This issue will be discussed in Chapter 5.

Here we wish to get a general picture of the level of consensus and conflict pertaining to various aspects of the race issue. We begin by looking at responses to seven questions asked in the 1968 SRC survey. The distribution of responses to these items is presented in Table 2.5.

The first three items pertain to government involvement in three areas of racial integration and equality—jobs, schools, and public accommodation. In each instance the question asked is whether or not the federal government should get involved or stay out. In each of the areas the government, through legislation, court decisions, or executive actions, has been involved. Although the extent of commitment and the amount of effort put out to implement policies and goals in these fields are questionable, the official policy of the national government lies in support of school integration, equal public accommodations, and equal job opportunities. On none of these three issues is there a consensus. On the job opportunity and school integration issues the pros and cons are closely divided, with neither position obtaining even a simple majority. On the right to go to any hotel and restaurant issue there is somewhat more support for government involvement, with 59 percent of the respondents maintaining that the government should get involved.

On each of these issues there is considerable division over the proposition of governmental involvement. The Survey Research Center has asked a question concerning whether or not the federal government should be involved in the school integration issue since 1956. The respondents have been very closely divided in their responses to that item in each of the surveys. At no point from 1956 through 1968 has the range between those favoring and those opposing government involvement been more than 10 percentage points. Although the margins of support and opposition have remained constant, it is likely that the meaning or interpretation of the question has changed. In 1956

TABLE 2.5   Opinions on race relations and civil rights issues, 1968

	Involvement of Federal Government		
1. Responses	JOBS[a]	SCHOOLS[b]	PUBLIC ACCOMMODATION[c]
Federal government should	44% (593)	43% (593)	59% (812)
Depends	7% (99)	8% (103)	3% (38)
Federal government should not	49% (663)	50% (681)	38% (517)

2. Neighborhood segregation
Which of these statements would you agree with?

Statement	% Agreeing With
Whites have right to keep blacks out of neighborhoods.	24% (341)
Negroes have right to live anywhere.	76% (1055)

3. Position on segregation[d]

Position Favored	% Choosing Position
Desegregation	37% (545)
In between	47% (699)
Segregation	16% (236)

4. Amount of change in position of Negro[e]

Position	% Choosing Position
A lot	50% (774)
Some	35% (539)
Not Much	15% (223)

5. Civil rights leaders pushing too fast?[f]

Position	% Choosing Position
Too fast	65% (957)
About right	28% (420)
Too slowly	7% (104)

Source: Data from 1968 SRC survey.

[a]The wording of the question was: Some people feel that if Negroes are not getting fair treatment in jobs, the government in Washington should see to it that they do. Others feel that this is not the federal government's business. Have you had enough interest in this question to favor one side over the other? Should the government in Washington . . .?"

[b] The wording of the question was: "Some people say that the government in Washington should see to it that white and Negro children are allowed to go to the same schools. Others claim that this is not the government's business. Have you been concerned enough about this question to favor one side over the other? (If yes) Do you think the government in Washington should . . .?"

[c] The wording of the question was: "As you may know, Congress passed a bill that says that Negroes should have the right to go to any hotel or restaurant they can afford, just like anyone else. Some people feel that this is something the government in Washington should support. Others feel that the government should stay out of this matter. Have you been interested enough in this to favor one side over the other?"

the question of the federal government getting involved in school integration probably meant, for most people, federal effort at doing away with the legally segregated school systems in the South. In the late sixties and early seventies the question is likely to connote, for many, redistricting school boundaries, consolidating districts, and bussing to bring about racial balance.

On the housing issue there appears to be a strong consensus in favor of the rights of blacks to live anywhere they want. Less than a quarter of the respondents affirm that whites have the right to keep blacks out of their neighborhoods. It should be noted that this question refers to abstract rights, not to the issue of governmental action or intervention as was the case with the previous three items. It does not ask directly about open housing legislation. A Gallup poll conducted in October 1968, about the same time as the SRC survey from which these data are taken, did ask respondents whether they favored or opposed "open housing" laws. Responses to this item were fairly equally divided, with 42 percent in favor, 37 percent opposed, and 27 percent with no opinion. [19]

The fifth question in Table 2.5 inquires into yet another aspect of race relations. It asks the respondent whether he favors desegregation, strict segregation, or something in between. The responses to this item indicate the ambivalence of many toward the issue of race relations. The proportion of persons affirming that they believe in strict segregation is quite small. On the other hand, only slightly more than a third of those responding indicate that they favor desegregation. The most widely chosen category, with almost 50 percent, is "something in between." It would seem that for one reason or another most Americans do not endorse, or feel that they should not endorse, strict segregation. On the other hand, they fall short of outright endorsement

----

[d] The wording of the question was: "Are you in favor of desegregation, strict segregation, or something in between?"

[e] The wording of the question was: "In the past few years we have heard a lot about civil rights groups working to improve the position of the Negro in this country. How much real change do you think there has been in the position of the Negro in the past few years: a lot, some, or not much at all?"

[f] The wording of the question was: "Some say that the civil rights people have been trying to push too fast. Others feel that they haven't pushed fast enough. How about you: Do you think that civil rights leaders are trying to push too fast, are going too slowly, or are they moving about the right speed?"

of desegregation. Desegregation may suggest to many various policies for forced integration such as bussing and racial hiring quotas, which tend to be unpopular. Torn between the two undesirable positions they identify themselves as somewhere in between.

The remaining two items in Table 2.5 pertain to the amount and speed of change in race relations. The sixth question asks the respondent how much change in the position of Negroes has taken place over the past few years. Half of the respondents report that a lot of change has taken place. Slightly more than a third say "some." Only 15 percent think that "not much" change had taken place. There seems to be consensus that at least some change has taken place, but no overall agreement that there has been a lot of change. In regard to the question of whether civil rights people have been trying to push too fast, a good majority (65 percent) chose the "too fast" response. A very small 7 percent reported feeling that civil rights leaders were pushing too slowly. Responses to Gallup polls taken during the same general period found similar distributions of responses to questions asking whether the administration (in those cases, the Johnson administration) was pushing integration too fast. It would seem that the majority of Americans think that changes in the condition of the black have been taking place and feel that at the present time change is being pushed too fast both by the government and by civil rights leaders.

The American public is very divided over the issues pertaining to racial equality and racial integration. In regard to some issues, conflict has been quite intense and has persisted over a number of years. The structure of attitudes and conflict on race is complex and defies simple designations. In regard to questions dealing with abstract rights and equality of opportunity there have been substantial changes in the outlooks of white Americans over the past three decades. There is probably a broad-based consensus in support of such notions as blacks being permitted to vote, being allowed to live where they want, and given equal opportunities for advancement. When it comes to government activities designed to assure equality and to bring about racial integration, however, the situation is quite different. There is no consensus in support of forced integration of schools, housing, neighborhoods, or for the enforcement of racial quotas requiring preferential treatment for minority groups in jobs, schools, and other groups. Although most Americans believe that change in the position of the black has taken place in the past few years and are willing to accept many areas of change, there seems to be widespread resentment about the speed of change and about the tactics used to bring about change in race relations and conditions.

The issue of race and race relations has been and will remain one of the most significant areas of social and political conflict in American society. Feelings of concern and assessment of personal and group interest are often very intense. Solutions to many of the problems and issues underlying racial tensions are not easy. The question of race has also become very much intertwined with most other questions and issues of contemporary society—welfare policies, crime and public order, the role and structure of educational institutions, boundaries of political units, unemployment, and attitudes toward the trust and responsiveness of government.

PUBLIC ORDER

During the past decade concern over public order, often designated the law and order issue, has emerged as a major political controversy. A nation that had viewed its political and social life as peaceful, orderly, and generally adhering to established political channels and procedures has been confronted by numerous instances of political violence—assassinations, riots, and sabotage. The use of "irregular" channels for the expression of political values and interests has become common-place. The issue of public order has many dimensions and origins. On the one hand, it entails rising crime rates and how governments should deal with them. It includes the disturbances that stem from racial tensions and frustrations. The demonstrations and disruptions connected with the Vietnam war have been an important part of it. Disturbances on college campuses, which were related to Vietnam and race, as well as to issues related to the schools themselves, have been major concerns. Lastly, the behavior and morals of young people, particularly the use of drugs, are an important component of the public order issue.

Political issues pertaining to public order have become important to many people. They have become an additional source of divisiveness and conflict. A Gallup poll taken in the spring of 1971 suggests the seriousness of concern for these problems. Nearly half of the respondents (47 percent) were concerned about the unrest and ill feeling between groups and thought it likely that they would "lead to a real breakdown in this country." [20] In addition to conflicts related to race and Vietnam, the public order or law and order issues have generated disputes over how to deal with disruptions and lawlessness as well as over the proper limits of dissent and rights of those accused of illegal acts. Opinion distributions for four public order type issues are presented in Table 2.6.

One of the most important conflicts regarding how to deal with unrest and disruptions is that of the use of force versus an emphasis upon trying to understand and deal with the reasons behind them. In regard to specific disruptions and more particular questions the public often seems prone to take a hard line, strongly supporting the use of force and harsh punishments. Two items from recent SRC election studies suggest, however, that the population is more evenly divided when more general questions are posed—issues divorced from particular disruptions (see Table 2.6). In the 1968 survey respondents were asked what they thought was the best approach in dealing with urban unrest. They were asked to place themselves on a seven-point scale with "solve problems of poverty and unemployment" at one end and "use all available force" at the other end. Of those answering, 41 percent placed themselves at the "solve poverty" end of the scale; 30 percent chose the position exactly in the middle; 30 percent placed themselves at the "use force" end. These responses suggest a public that is divided over how to deal with the problem of public order. In response to a question asking whether people sympathized with students and faculty or thought schools should use force to stop rioting and disturbances on college campuses and high schools, posed in the 1970 SRC survey, 17 percent leaned toward sympathy with students and faculty, 18 percent placed themselves in the middle, and 66 percent leaned toward the use of force. These responses suggest that there is less sympathy for the protests of students than for the frustrations of ghetto blacks who are most closely associated with urban riots.

In order to ascertain feelings toward the use of "irregular" channels of political expression, respondents were asked in the 1968 SRC survey whether or not they approved people showing dissatisfaction with government by "taking part in protest meetings or marches that are permitted by the local authorities." Slightly over half of those who responded reported that they disapproved; 20 percent expressed

TABLE 2.6 Opinion on public order issues, 1968 and 1970

1. Best way to deal with urban unrest (1968)[a]		
1. Solve unemployment and poverty	20%	(249)
2.	11%	(142)
3.	10%	(129)
4.	29%	(372)
5.	10%	(126)
6.	8%	(97)
7. Use all available force	12%	(153)
2. Response to campus unrest (1970)[b]		
1. Sympathize with students and faculty	6%	(79)
2.	5%	(66)
3.	6%	(81)
4.	18%	(244)
5.	11%	(148)
6.	15%	(206)
7. Use force	41%	(569)
3. Attitude toward demonstrations and protests (1968)[c]		
Approve	20%	(242)
Depends	27%	(334)
Disapprove	54%	(664)
4. Emphasis in dealing with accused (1970)[d]		
1. Protect rights of accused	19%	(246)
2.	8%	(99)
3.	7%	(90)
4.	17%	(225)
5.	12%	(159)
6.	15%	(188)
7. Do anything necessary to stop crime	22%	(286)

Source: Data from SRC surveys, 1968, 1970.

[a] Question was: "There is much discussion about the best way to deal with the problem of urban unrest and rioting. Some say it is more important to use all available force to maintain law and order—no matter what results. Others say it is more important to correct the problems of poverty and unemployment that give rise to the disturbances. And, of course, other people have opinions in between. Suppose the people who stress the use of force are at one end of this scale—at point number 7. And suppose the people who stress doing more about the problems of poverty and unemployment are at the other end—at point number 1. Where would you place yourself on this scale?" (1968 SRC survey).

[b] Question was: "Some people are pretty upset about rioting and disturbances on college campuses and in high schools. Some feel sympathetic with the students and faculty who take part in these disturbances. Others think the schools should use police and the national guard to prevent or stop disturbances. And others fall somewhere between these extremes. Where would you place yourself on this scale, or haven't you thought much about this?" (1970 SRC survey).

[c] Question was: "How about taking part in protest meetings or marches that are permitted by the local authorities? Would you approve of doing that, disapprove, or would it depend on the circumstances?" (1968 SRC survey).

[d] Question was: "Some people are primarily concerned with doing everything possible to protect the legal rights of those accused of committing crimes. Others feel that it is more important to stop criminal activity even at the risk of reducing the rights of the accused. Where would you place yourself on this scale, or haven't you thought much about this?" (1970 SRC survey).

approval; and 27 percent said it would depend. Relatively few people expressed outright approval even of "legal" demonstrations.

The concern with rising crime rates, coupled with a series of Supreme Court decisions protecting the rights of the accused in criminal court proceedings, have led to another issue of contention in the law and order area. This has to do with the relative weight placed on safeguarding the rights of those accused of crime versus the pressure to obtain convictions in criminal proceedings in order to protect the safety of the public. A question asked in the 1970 SRC survey found the public very much divided on where emphasis should be placed. The question, like some of the others, asked the respondent to place himself on a seven-point scale with "protect the rights of accused" at one end and "stop crime regardless of rights of accused" at the other end. Of the respondents, 37 percent placed themselves in one of the three points leaning toward the "protection of rights" end; 49 percent leaned toward the other end; 17 percent chose the midpoint position.

There are numerous other dimensions of the public order issue that could be discussed. These items, however, ought to be sufficient to give the reader a general notion of the controversies related to the public order issue and the distributions of opinions in regard to some of them. It is an area in which feelings and fears are often intense and one that is closely intertwined with other issues and conflicts. It served as an important, though often vaguely articulated, issue in the 1968, 1970, and 1972 national elections.

GOVERNMENTAL TRUST AND RESPONSIVENESS

The new and intense issue conflicts and the response of the political system to them have led to another area of concern: the responsiveness and trustworthiness of government. Feelings about government have become a primary area of concern. The term "credibility gap," which has been applied to both the Johnson and Nixon administrations, is one popular manifestation of this concern. Attitudes toward government and politics constitute a key aspect of the basic political malaise discussed in Chapter 1. In a period in which people are strongly agitated about many issues and in which citizen participation is a key political slogan, it is not strange that concern with political responsiveness should be significant. In a time of considerable conflict over new issues and the absence of stable issue and group coalitions it is not strange that government and political leaders find it difficult to respond.

Several questions related to people's feelings about the trustworthiness and responsiveness of the government were asked in the SRC 1968 survey. The questions and distributions of responses are shown in Table 2.7. The responses, as a whole, suggest both disagreement among the population and considerable distrust. By a large margin, respondents think that political parties do not keep their promises, yet by almost exactly the same 2 to 1 margin they think that elections affect government policy a good deal. This suggests a curious combination of cynicism about political parties and optimism concerning the impact of elections. Only a quarter of the respondents thought that the government pays a good deal of attention to what people think in making decisions. But slightly less than half felt that it paid some attention.

On the two other items, the trust of government to do what is right and whether the government works for the benefit of all or a few big interests, the respondents are more evenly divided. These two items have been used in four SRC surveys, running from 1964 through 1970. A comparison of responses to the two items over time suggests that a substantial shift toward more negative attitudes has occurred over the six-year time span. The trend toward negative responses over the four election studies is as follows:

	1964	1966	1968	1970	change 1964 to 1970
% saying government can be trusted only some or none of time	22%	32%	37%	45%	+23
% saying government works for benefit of few big interests	30%	36%	41%	55%	+25

TABLE 2.7   Opinions concerning governmental trust and responsiveness, 1968

1. Political parties keep promises [a]		
Keep their promises	30%	(394)
Depends	7%	(90)
Do what they want	63%	(825)
2. Elections make government pay attention to people [b]		
A good deal	62%	(799)
Some	30%	(382)
Not much	9%	(112)
3. Government pays attention to what people think [c]		
A good deal	25%	(310)
Some	45%	(562)
Not much	31%	(390)
4. Trust government to do what is right [d]		
Always	8%	(98)
Most of the time	55%	(724)
Some of the time	37%	(486)
None of the time	0%	(2)
5. Government benefits all or few [e]		
For benefit of all	54%	(684)
Few big interests	41%	(528)
Depends	5%	(66)

Source: Data from SRC 1968 survey.

[a] Question was: "Do you think that the parties will keep their promises or do they usually do what they want after the election is over?"

[b] Question was: "And how much do you feel that having elections makes the government pay attention to what the people think: a good deal, some, or not much?"

[c] Question was: "Over the years, how much attention do you feel the government pays to what people think when it decides what to do: a good deal, some, or not much?"

[d] Question was: "How much of the time do you think that you can trust the government in Washington to do what is right—just about always, most of the time, or only some of the time?"

[e] Question was: "Would you say the government is pretty much run by a few big interests looking out for themselves or that it is run for the benefit of all people?"

These trend figures suggest a steady and considerable erosion of trust in the government. The proportion of persons reporting that the government can be trusted only some or none of the time more than doubled. The increase in those saying the government works primarily for the benefit of the few fell only slightly short of doubling. By 1970 the population was almost evenly split on both of the items.

Many Americans have developed serious doubts about whether their traditional institutions and current leadership are able and/or interested in coping with the current problems confronting the nation. As was reported above, nearly half of those responding to a Gallup survey in the spring of 1971 thought that current unrest and group hostilities were likely to lead to a "real breakdown in this country." When the respondents were asked to choose which one or two of a list of six reasons were mainly responsible for the unrest and ill feeling, the most commonly chosen response was: "Our traditional way of doing things is not working and some basic changes are needed if we are to work together." Of these respondents 34 percent chose this response; 31 percent chose "Our leaders in government and business are not trying hard enough to solve the problems we face and people are losing confidence in them" as one of their main reasons.

CONCLUSIONS

This overview of contemporary political opinions suggests a number of important facets of conflict and consensus. First, the politics of consensus, a key theme of political commentators during the mid-1960s and the condition projected by Lane as the political consequence of affluence, is not the political reality in the early 1970s. A dampening of the cleavages centering around welfare state propositions and the development of a widespread consensus in support of a wide range of economic welfare and industrial relations policies may have occurred, in a manner like that suggested by Lane. However, new areas of political conflict have arisen instead of the general consensus. In the area of race relations the public remains very much divided over policies concerning racial integration and equal opportunities. Abstract notions of equality and justice may be generally agreed upon, but the government actions and pressure from minority groups to bring about integration and equality evoke considerable controversy. The involvement in Vietnam has created serious conflicts and mistrust that are not likely to disappear very rapidly. A wide spectrum of issues pertaining to the general issue of public order have also come to divide the public, generating animosities that are often rather bitter. In addition to the many policy issues over which there are substantial divisions, there appears to be a significant and growing disaffection from American politics and government. There has been a significant growth in mistrust of government and in pessimism over the ability of government and political leaders to cope with current problems and issues.

The existence of these several areas of widely divided opinions over issues that are of primary political concern—especially the newer type issues such as race, the involvement in Vietnam, and public order— suggests a period of considerable political conflict and social division. These new issues and conflicts are not likely to be ameliorated by affluence, as may have been the case with some of the conflicts centering around the issues of economic welfare and industrial regulation. In fact, affluence may in some instances have helped give rise to these new tensions and cleavages. Student dissenters and youthful dropouts have tended to be products of more affluent families and neighborhoods. Lubell argues that some aspects of recent urban racial tensions have been facilitated by the improved economic conditions of many blacks. Better incomes and higher aspirations have allowed them to move out of old ghetto areas and into new previously white neighborhoods, and thus pose a threat to some whites in a way they did not when they were less economically well off or mobile.

As we discuss in more detail later, these new conflicts tend not to follow the traditional structures of political cleavage. Opinions on these new issues do not readily divide along the lines of haves and have-nots. The divisions often center around values and morals, around different life-styles and world views which seem to have little relationship with the more traditional social divisions. This may make them particularly unsusceptible to easy solution, especially through the conventional patterns of incrementalism, bargaining, and compromise which have characterized American politics.

Notes

[1] See V. O. Key, Jr., *Public Opinion and American Democracy* (New York: Knopf, 1963), chapters 2 and 3, for a discussion of patterns of consensus and conflict in American politics.

[2] Alexis de Tocqueville, *Democracy in America*, vol. I (New York: Vintage Books, 1945), p. 334.

[3] John K. Galbraith, *The Affluent Society* (Boston: Houghton Mifflin, 1958).

[4] Robert E. Lane, "The Politics of Consensus in an Age of Affluence," *American Political Science Review*, LIX (December 1965), pp. 874–895.

[5] Ibid., p. 874.

[6] Ibid., p. 877.

[7] The year 1956 was the first SRC election survey in which a substantial number of policy questions were asked. Other survey data on general issues areas are sparse for the early 1950s.

[8] Lloyd A. Free and Hadley Cantril, *The Political Beliefs of Americans* (New York: Simon and Schuster, 1968).

[9] Ibid., p. 16.

[10] *Gallup Political Index* (Princeton, N.J.: Gallup International).

[11] *Gallup Political Index*, No. 47 (May 1969), p. 15.

[12] *Gallup Political Index*, No. 50 (August 1969), p. 19.

[13] *Gallup Political Index*, No. 43 (January 1969), p. 20.

[14] Ibid., p. 21.

[15] *Gallup Political Index* (1966–1970).

[16] *Gallup Political Index*, No. 77 (November 1971).

[17] AIPO (December 1968), p. 773; (July 1969), p. 784, and (March 1971), p. 825.

[18] The extent to which the Vietnam issue continued to severely and closely divide the population in 1972 can be seen in public responses to the issue of escalating the bombing of North Vietnam in the spring of 1972. A Gallup poll found that 47 percent were in favor of the increased bombing and 44 percent opposed it. *Gallup Political Index*, No. 83 (May 1972), p. 21.

[19] *Gallup Political Index*, No. 40 (October 1968), p. 31.

[20] Albert H. Cantril and Charles W. Roll, Jr., *Hopes and Fears of the American People* (New York: Universe Books, 1971), p. 33.

CHAPTER 3
ISSUE SALIENCY AND
INTERRELATIONSHIP OF OPINIONS

A decade ago terms such as Vietnam, ecological crisis, credibility gap, forced bussing, white backlash, New Left, hard hats, black power, and acidheads were not familiar to most Americans. They played no part in shaping the political consciousness. Over the past decade these concepts have become a significant aspect of American political life. They are terms that evoke intense feelings and serve as subjects for heated political debates. The focus and concerns of American political life have changed considerably in less than a decade. The shift in concerns and the emergence of new issues have led to new divisions and patterns of conflict. These changes are an important aspect of the current political disarray.

An understanding of the nature and consequences of issue conflict requires knowing more than how many people hold what opinions on given issues. One also must know how important various issues are for people and the extent of their political relevance. In addition it is important to know something about how the distributions of opinions in various issue areas are related to opinion distributions in other issue areas. Are people who have opposed the involvement in Vietnam likely to support or to oppose government medical assistance? Does support for school integration go hand in hand with higher or with lower levels of political trust? Or are these two sets of issue opinions not related? Do "liberal" attitudes concerning government welfare involvement tend to be associated with "liberal" attitudes regarding demonstrations and the right to political dissent. We suggest in the previous chapters that along with the changes in issue concern there have been changes in the issue coalitions and opinion cluster.

In this chapter we first look at what changes have taken place in issue focus over the past few years. Then we discuss how opinions in the several issue areas developed in the last chapter relate to each other.

CHANGES IN POLITICALLY SALIENT ISSUES

One of the important propositions of this analysis is that there have been changes in recent years in what issues are politically important, or salient, to Americans. Issues and questions that were nonexistent or of little political concern a few years back have become key areas of political focus and controversy. Race, Vietnam, crime in the street, public order, ecology, and the reordering of societal goals and priorities (if issue-oriented political groups and the communication media are appropriate indicators) have been widely discussed political issues.

A salient political issue has two major characteristics. First, it is an issue that large numbers of people are concerned about, something they consider important and feel involved with. Second, it is relevant politically. People associate it and the handling of it with the political process and political leaders.

The population can be greatly divided over an issue, or united in support of some proposition, without that issue being salient. For example, during the early 1950s one issue before Congress was the admission of Alaska and Hawaii as states in the Union. Public opinion polls suggested that there was a strong consensus in favor of admission and had been for some time.[1] However, the admission issue was not an important or salient concern for most people. It was not an issue over which people got very agitated or around which they made political evaluations and choices. Key suggests that public opinion constituted what he calls a permissive consensus.[2] People in general supported statehood but did not care much one way or the other whether it was accomplished. The government and political leaders, then, were free to act or not to act. The issue was political, but it was not salient.

Religious issues, in general, represent a contrary situation. A theological question such as whether or not there actually is a heaven or a hell may be an issue upon which believers are divided. People may be very much concerned about the questions and their consequences. Many people may have a high sense of personal stake and personal involvement in questions pertaining to an afterlife. For most Americans, however, religious doctrinal issues such as these are not *politically* salient. People generally do not look toward political leaders and political processes to resolve such questions. With respect to these issues the agitation and concern may be present, but the political relevance is not.

Issues of race relations and racial equality today are very much politically salient issues. They are problems about which many people have a great deal of concern and, often, a sense of personal as well as national stake in the outcomes. They are politically relevant inasmuch as people increasingly have come to look toward, and even to pressure the government to intervene in one way or another. Race has not always been a salient political issue for most of the public.[3] The concentration of blacks in the South until the past few decades, the federal system which allowed many of the policy issues for which race has particular relevance to be handled by the states, and a lack of concern among most Americans with issues of racial equality and racial justice kept the race question from becoming a salient national political issue through much of our history. The greater dispersal of the black population; the increased intervention of the federal government into areas of education, social welfare, and economic regulation; changing sociological and moral concepts concerning race; and the development of a political consciousness among blacks have all worked together to make race relations an area of salient political concern.

The types of issues that are of particular concern to the public have varied over time. There are both short-run and long-run variations in issue concern. Issues such as what languages should be used in public schools, programs promoting internal improvements and the settlement of the western frontier, and the prohibition of liquor were very salient political concerns for many people during various periods in the nineteenth century. They are not of urgent public concern today. Controlling industrial pollution, limiting population growth, and controlling the level of defense spending were not salient issues during most of the early nineteenth century. They are issues of some political importance today. If public opinion data were available it might be possible to trace precisely basic changes in issue saliency over long time periods. It seems apparent that different historical periods have had different sets of problems and issues that have been particularly salient to the people at the time. Ladd, in his analysis of American political parties, developed a notion of American development in terms of "sociopolitical" periods. Each of these periods has had its particular "political agenda" around which form political coalitions and conflicts.[4] Changes in these political agendas constitute what we refer to as long-run changes in political issue saliency.

Short-run fluctuations also take place within the socio-political periods. During periods of international crisis, of war or the threat of war, people become concerned about international issues and foreign policy. During those periods foreign policy and national defense issues may become salient for many. As the crisis subsides, foreign policy and defense concerns may become less important to most people. Similar fluctuations can be expected with respect to economic conditions. During times of economic recession or inflation people become particularly concerned about the state of the economy. During more prosperous and economically stable times their central concerns may be elsewhere. This appears to have been the case in the United States in the early 1970s. Throughout the mid and late 1960s general economic conditions were seldom mentioned as a major important problem facing the country. In 1971, with inflation and unemployment both on the rise, however, the economy became a top concern.

The late 1960s and early 1970s appear to be a time of transition in long-run basic issue focus. The questions of economic security and of economic and industrial regulation which were the central political concerns over most of the first half of the twentieth century seem to be of less intense concern today. As we suggested in the preceding chapter, a general broad consensus in support of basic welfare state programs and propositions seems to have developed by the late 1950s and early 1960s. These types of issues have been stressed relatively less in national elections since 1964, except where the Democratic party has stressed its role over the past few decades in bringing about measures contributing to social and economic security and general prosperity. The economic security and industrial regulation issues seem less significant as sources of political cleavages than they were in the previous few decades.

Other issues, other sources of political divisions and cleavages are beginning to emerge. Scammon and Wattenberg in their book *The Real Majority* talk about these changes in terms of the rise of what they call the "social issue," a series of problems distinct from the more traditional "economic issue." [5] The social issue includes the questions of public order, crime and lawlessness, and many aspects of the race issue, which we discussed in the preceding chapter. Lane's basic thesis about the political consequences of affluence also suggests that there will be a waning of concern and involvement with the more traditional economic and industrial relations issues. As we suggested in the last chapter, however, Lane's argument does not predict the emergence of new areas of political and social conflict.

It is difficult to obtain precise measures of issue salience and concerns within the general population. The focus of political campaigns and themes stressed in the mass media may not always reflect what the general public is thinking. It is particularly difficult to trace trends in issue importance over time. Gallup polls and SRC election surveys, however, have asked questions pertaining to what people think are the important problems facing the country. Since 1960, SRC studies have included a question asking respondents: "What do you personally feel are the most important problems which the government in Washington should try to take care of?"—with only slight variations in wording. A look at trends in the responses to this question over the short time span from 1960 through 1970 provides some insight into what the major focus of concerns has been and what changes in emphasis have taken place over the past decade.

The responses to this question as asked in the 1960, 1964, and 1968 presidential election surveys are presented in Table 3.1. Responses from the 1970 off-year elections are also included to provide a more recent reading. The data in Table 3.1 pertain to the first most important problem identified by the respondent. The data represent the relative frequency of first choices falling in each of eight general problem categories.

The data suggest a number of trends relevant to the developments with which we are concerned here. By far the most significant change over time is the substantial increase in concern for race and public order type issues. In 1960 only 6 percent of the respondents mentioned race or public order issues as the first most important problem. In 1964, 18 percent mentioned race or public order issues, and in 1968, 27 percent indicated primary concern with problems that fell in that category. The relative frequency of race-public order mentions stays about the same from 1968 to 1970. In less than a decade race or public order concerns

TABLE 3.1 Changes 1960–1970 in most important problems[a]

Problem	1960	1964	1968	1970
1. Social Welfare	13%	20%	12%	16%
2. Agriculture-Natural Resources	5	2	1	6
3. Labor	2	1	1	1
4. Race-Public Order	6	18	27	24
5. Economic, Business, Consumer	8	7	6	13
6. Foreign Affairs	49	26	48	33
7. National Defense	6	5	1	1
8. Functioning of Government	0	2	2	3
No Problem Mentioned	11	20	3	4

Source: Data from SRC surveys, 1960, 1964, 1968, 1970.
[a] The percentages represent the relative frequencies with which problems falling in the several categories were mentioned as the *first* most important problem in each of the four years.

grew from one of the least numerous responses to second place, with only Vietnam ranking above it in 1968 and 1970.

The proportion of respondents mentioning foreign policy issues as the first most important problem varies considerably from year to year. Foreign policy responses were most numerous in 1960 and least numerous in 1964. They were high in 1968 but dropped off considerably two years later. The types of foreign policy problems, however, changed considerably between the two high points in 1960 and 1968. A very substantial part of the foreign policy problems mentioned in 1968 had to do with Vietnam, which was not an important concern in 1960. The 1960 foreign policy responses are scattered among a wide range of specific issues. Many of them centered around cold war issues and military competition with the Soviet Union. At that time cold war tensions were high, and Kennedy, the Democratic candidate for president, made the missile gap and insufficient effort for national defense major campaign issues. In 1970, as in 1968, a substantial proportion of the foreign policy responses had to do with Vietnam. Thus, the drop-off between 1968 and 1970 in the foreign policy category represents a decrease in focus on Vietnam. In 1968 nearly half of the respondents mentioned the war as the most important problem. In 1970 that number had decreased to somewhat less than a third (29 percent).

The frequency with which the more traditional economic and

industrial relations problems are cited follows a still different pattern. Throughout the period relatively few respondents mentioned labor and union-management problems. Concern for problems in the field of social welfare was highest in 1964. Social security, medical assistance for aged, and poverty were mentioned by a number of people. That was the year that Goldwater ran as the Republican candidate and made social security and other welfare state policies into campaign issues. The citing of agricultural-natural resource problems decreased from 1960 to 1968 but returned to the 1960 level in 1970. Again, the broad category hides significant change. In 1960 the bulk of the responses falling in the agriculture-natural resources category had to do with farm problems. In 1970 they constitute concern for pollution and the environment.

Increases in the social welfare and in economic, business, and consumer categories between 1968 and 1970 represent concern over the state of the economy, rather than more general concern with welfare and industrial relations issues. Both rising inflation and rising unemployment had become acute problems by 1970. References to unemployment were coded under social welfare, and references to inflation and business conditions were included under economic, business, and consumer problems. We would expect that the upswing in the citing of social welfare and economic problems reflects a particular concern for specific economic conditions, rather than a swing toward greater focus on general economic welfare and industrial relations issues. That is, the changes between 1968 and 1970 represent the type of short-term fluctuations we discussed above, rather than long-term shifts.

One additional trend suggested by the data in Table 3.1 is worth mentioning; that is, the change over time in the number of persons who fail to mention a single important problem. In 1968 and 1970, 3 and 4 percent, respectively, did not mention a problem. In 1960, 11 percent mentioned no issue. In 1964 almost 1 out of 5 failed to mention a problem. These findings provide additional evidence for a point made in Chapter 1. Over the past years citizens have been unusually interested in and concerned about issues. This pattern is also an interesting commentary on the relationships between political problems, political campaigns, and public opinion. The 1964 presidential campaign was the one in which the Republican candidate sought to make the electoral contest "a choice and not an echo," one in which issues were discussed and confronted more than has usually been the case, and one in which the candidates often took divergent positions on issues. In connection with that election there was the highest proportion of respondents unable to mention even one important problem. In 1968, on the other hand, a year in which parties and candidates tended to avoid strong, concrete issue positions and to play down important areas of conflict, almost none of the respondents was unable to mention a most important problem. Looking at the situation from another perspective, 1964 and, to a lesser extent, 1960 were years in which the people were not particularly agitated over issues and problems. To some extent the campaigns and candidates worked to create and to sell issue concerns. The missile gap concern in 1960 is a good example. In 1968, as Lubell pointed out in *The Hidden Crisis in American Politics*, the voters were unusually agitated and concerned about some specific issues. In that election candidates sought to play down issues and mute conflicts.

Gallup polls which have asked respondents what they thought were the most important problems show a similar emphasis on the issues of Vietnam, race, and crime-public order problems over the past six years—with the economy coming up in 1970 and 1971. The ordered rankings of the most often mentioned problems for a selection of polls from 1965 through 1971 are presented in Table 3.2. These will enable the reader to see more clearly the comparative rankings of problems during the period under discussion. From 1965 through mid-1971 Vietnam is almost always the most frequently cited problem. Throughout 1965 and 1966 civil rights and race relations generally rank in second place. The issues of crime and related problems such as youth demonstrations and other disturbances take second place to Vietnam through most of 1968 and 1969. In March 1968, however, crime and lawlessness climbed into first place, as did campus disorders in the summer of 1970. In 1970 the economic issue (inflation, unemployment, etc.) had become important, vying with race and crime for second place. By the spring of 1971 the *Gallup Opinion Index* reported that public concern over the economy was greater than at any time since the 1958 recession, when unemployment was named the most important problem in the nation.[6] Concern over the condition of the

TABLE 3.2 Trends in most important problems Gallup polls 1965-1971

1. June 1965*		
1. Vietnam	23%	
2. Civil Rights	23%	
3. Threat of War	16%	
4. Prestige Abroad	9%	
5. Spread of World Communism	9%	
2. October 1965		
1. Civil Rights	27%	
2. Vietnam	19%	
3. Threat of War	17%	
4. Prestige Abroad	7%	
5. Spread of World Communism	6%	
3. November 1965		
1. Vietnam Crisis	37%	
2. Civil Rights	17%	
3. Threat of War	7%	
4. Prestige Abroad	6%	
5. High Cost of Living	6%	
4. December 1965		
1. Vietnam	33%	
2. Civil Rights	19%	
3. Threat of World War III	11%	
4. Threat of World Communism	9%	
5. Prestige High Cost of Living	5%	
5. September 1966		
1. International (Vietnam)	56%	
2. Racial Problems	24%	
3. High Cost of Living	16%	

6. May 1968		
1. Vietnam	42%	
2. Race Relations	25%	
3. Crime, Lawlessness	15%	
4. High Cost of Living	8%	
5. Poverty	4%	
7. July 1968		
1. Vietnam	52%	
2. Crime, Lawlessness	29%	
3. Race	13%	
4. High Cost	9%	
5. Poverty	3%	
8. August 1968		
1. Vietnam	51%	
2. Crime, Lawlessness	21%	
3. Race	20%	
4. High Cost	7%	
5. Poverty	3%	
9. October 1968		
1. Vietnam	44%	
2. Crime	25%	
3. Race	17%	
4. High Cost	6%	
10. March 1969		
1. Vietnam	40%	
2. Crime	17%	
3. Race	16%	
4. Inflation	9%	
5. College Demonstration	4%	

11. Summer 1969

		1st
1.	Vietnam	40%
2.	Youth Demonstration	15%
3.	Civil Rights	12%
4.	Inflation	6%
5.	Crime	6%
6.	Pollution, Ecology	6%
7.	Drug Addiction	8%
8.	Division in America, Polarization of View	8%
9.	Poverty, Welfare	2%
10.	Education	2%
11.	Lack of Religion, Moral Decay	2%
12.	Other Responses	7%
13.	No Opinion	4%
		107%

Table adds to more than 100% because of multiple responses.

12. February 1970

1.	Vietnam	33%
2.	High Cost of Living	17%
3.	Race Relations	13%
4.	Crime	7%
5.	Other International Problems	6%
6.	Drug-taking, Addiction	5%
7.	Poverty	5%
8.	Teenage Problems	4%
9.	Air & Water Pollution	4%
10.	Immorality, Lack of Religion	4%
11.	Educational Needs	2%
12.	Citizen Apathy	2%
13.	Others	3%
14.	No Opinion	2%
		107%

Table adds to more than 100% because of multiple answers.

13. September 1970

1.	Vietnam, Indochina	26%
2.	Economic	11%
3.	Other International	15%
4.	Crime, Lawlessness	5%
5.	Race Relations	11%

14. February 1971

1.	Vietnam, Indochina	28%
2.	Economic	24%
3.	Other International	12%
4.	Crime, Lawlessness	7%
5.	Race Relations	7%
6.	Pollution, Ecology	7%
7.	Drug Addiction	6%
8.	Division in America, Polarization of View	6%
9.	Poverty, Welfare	5%
10.	Education	2%
11.	Lack of Religion, Moral Decay	2%
12.	Other Responses	6%
13.	No Opinion	2%
		114%

Table adds to more than 100% because of multiple responses.

Source: Data from *Gallup Opinion Index* (1965–1971).
*Question asked "What do you think is the *most* important problem facing this country today?"

economy remained high through the remainder of 1971.

The data from both the SRC surveys and the Gallup polls support the contention that important new areas of political concern have developed over the past decade. Concern over the economy rose in the early 1970s in the wake of several years of adverse economic conditions, but that concern is probably particularistic. It is likely to subside, with improvements in the state of the economy. There seems little primary focus on the more traditional problems and programs dealing with economic security and industrial relations. On this point it is useful to note the pattern of responses to 1970 SRC issue questions in which respondents were presented with a list of nine policy issues and asked how important each issue was to the respondent. Out of nine issues asked about, the highest proportion of "not important" or "not very important" responses was given to the government health insurance question, the only traditional welfare type issue asked about in the series. It ranked in importance behind issues such as urban unrest, student disturbances, government aid to minority groups, pollution, and protecting the rights of those accused of crimes.

The focus on problems dealing with race and public order, whose development is indicated so clearly by the trend data, probably represents a more basic shift in social and political issue saliency. A wide constellation of issues pertaining to race are likely to be salient political issues for some time to come. The problems are fundamental. They are not apt to be solved quickly or simply. Although it will show its face in many different forms, concern with crime, lawlessness, political and social dissent, and public and personal morality, which fall under the general rubric of public order, also are likely to confront American politics for a number of years. The social, economic, and cultural changes taking place will continue to generate social tensions, public disorder, and conflicts in morals and behavior. The waning of economic and class-related tensions and issues, among other things, enables racial, cultural, and behavioral conflicts to assume center stage as foci of political interest and conflict.

Race, Vietnam, and public order have been not only the most politically salient issues. They also have been the issues over which the citizenry has been most deeply divided. The opinion distributions of the last chapter identified a number of areas of deep and persistent

division over race relations policy. Even though the military involvement in Southeast Asia has been brought to a close, that involvement
has created a series of divisions that will not be rapidly healed. Urban
riots, student unrest, crime, and the use of drugs, as well as questions
pertaining to both the causes of these behaviors and how they should
be dealt with, constitute yet another area of deepening divisions and
political concerns. The use of force versus dealing with the underlying
social and economic conditions causing crime and disorder represents
one key aspect of this conflict. The legalization of marijuana, abortion,
and homosexual relationships suggests another dimension. The many
tensions generated by race, Vietnam, and public order controversies,
changes in political values and expectations, and the sluggishness with
which the political system is able to respond to new concerns, have
precipitated anxiety and controversy over governmental trust and
responsiveness.

OPINION INTERRELATIONSHIPS

Vietnam, race, public order, and governmental trust have emerged as
important new political concerns and controversies in contemporary
American political life. They vie with economic welfare issues, more
traditional foreign policy concerns, and anxiety over the state of the
economy as the political issues of most concern to the public. The
distributions of opinions on a series of items in six major issue areas
were presented in the preceding chapter. The changing focus of issue
concern during the last decade has been discussed in the first part of
this chapter. We turn now to another important consideration, the
relationships between opinion distributions in different issue areas.

Do these several new issues divide the population in ways that are
similar to or dissimilar from one another? How do opinions on these
new issues relate to opinions on the more conventional economic
welfare-industrial relations issues, to opinions on traditional foreign
policy matters? Are there in the population new ideological syndromes
or common related political outlooks covering a wide range of issue
areas? Or does each of these issue areas have its particular independent
focus and unique opinion distribution? For example, are persons who
held a dovish position on the Vietnam involvement more likely than

hawks to be prointergration on race relations issues? Are they likely to be more opposed to a tough line on public order matters, and less trustful of government? How do positions on the newer issues relate to outlooks on the traditional welfare state issues and to more traditional international concerns such as isolationism? Stating the problem in another way, are we developing within the population large aggregates of people who share common outlooks over a wide range of issues? Or do we have shifting coalitions with shared opinions only within distinct issues areas?

Among the most popular terms used to identify large groupings of persons with common outlooks on a range of issues are the labels "liberal" and "conservative." These labels are widely used by political commentators, by political theorists, and by the public at large to indicate some type of general political outlook. In the political setting of the immediate post–World War II period it was generally held that Senator Robert Taft of Ohio was a conservative and Eleanor Roosevelt a liberal. In the 1950s Hubert Humphrey was regarded as a leading liberal and Barry Goldwater a conservative. Within limits these terms, as applied to political leaders such as these, indicated that person's position on a number of issues. The liberal was likely to be a supporter of organized labor and to support legislation favored by labor and of particular benefit to the working man. The conservative tended to be at odds with organized labor and on more friendly terms with the leaders and interests of business. Conservatives, such as Taft and Goldwater, were generally opposed to increasing the role of government in economic and industrial regulation. Liberals, such as Roosevelt and Humphrey, were more likely to support them. Although the distinctions were not always so clear with respect to international relations, one can say that, in general, the liberal leader was more likely to favor providing economic assistance to neutral nations that did not support U.S. policy and interests in the cold war and to favor negotiations with, rather than belligerency toward, the Soviet Union. Conservatives were more reluctant to aid neutralist nations and to place faith in the possibility of peaceful cooperation with the Soviets.

Today, even among political leaders, the terms liberal and conservative have taken on different meanings and have lost clarity and consistency. In the Democratic presidential race in 1972 George

McGovern was acclaimed as the liberal candidate. Senators Humphrey and Jackson were considered by many to be more conservative. Yet it was Humphrey and Jackson who were the acknowledged "friends" of labor. McGovern, because of his "liberal" positions on issues such as Vietnam and defense spending and because of some of his past votes on key labor legislation, was generally opposed by the leaders of organized labor and was not particularly popular among working-class voters. In the primaries Humphrey proved particularly popular among blacks and Jews, even though they have generally been among the most liberal groupings within the electorate. On the other hand, Humphrey was considered by many to be too conservative because he was not an early opponent of the Vietnam involvement and did not support large-scale cutbacks in defense spending. Senator Jackson, trying to appeal to the working-class vote, stressed the need for the government to do more to alleviate unemployment, a traditional liberal position. Yet he was regarded by many as the most conservative of the candidates because of his strong support of high defense expenditures and his opposition to the use of bussing for school integration.

These examples from the battle for the 1972 Democratic presidential nomination, in addition to suggesting the contemporary confusion surrounding the use of the terms liberal and conservative, also indicate the extent to which even among political leaders there do not appear to be very consistent interissue patterns. Wallace and McGovern may agree on the need for tax reform to decrease the burden on lower- and lower-middle-income families. They do not agree, however, on issues pertaining to race and public order. Humphrey and McGovern may agree on many policies pertaining to racial equality and integration, but not on policies pertaining to national defense and income redistribution. All of the 1972 Democratic contenders agreed on the need for more government assistance in the field of health care, but they espoused different approaches to the issues of public order and to questions of the legalization of marijuana and abortions.

With the rise of the newer divisive issues it has become increasingly difficult to apply the terms liberal and conservative in any meaningful way. Some now refer to "old liberals" as distinct from "new liberals." For old liberals the issue context has centered primarily around the traditional economic welfare and industrial relations area, with an emphasis on prolabor and prowelfare state positions. For new liberals the key issue concerns have been Vietnam, defense spending, aid to minorities, and the "new politics."

Despite the often confusing usage of the terms and the expansion of salient political issues there are popular comprehensive notions of what constitutes the liberal and the conservative in the population today. According to the common popular image, the liberal has opposed the involvement in Vietnam and favored rapid withdrawal and disengagement. He is highly supportive of racial integration and of government actions to advance the interests and well-being of minority groups, including the poor. He is tolerant of many types of public disorders, sympathetic to student and racial dissent, and opposed to the use of force as the basic tactic for coping with lawlessness and disorder. He has become increasingly distrustful of the government and its responsiveness to current problems and issues. On social welfare type issues he supports most policies extending welfare state type activities, especially those that benefit the poor and minority groups. He has become more hesitant about extensive U.S. involvement in world affairs, and favors cutbacks in defense spending and a general reordering of national priorities.

On the other side of the political spectrum, the conservative has supported the Vietnam involvement. He has been hostile toward those who dissent from government policy in Vietnam. He is negative about government policies directed toward racial integration—especially such programs as bussing, school reorganization, the forced dispersal of public housing, and racial quotas. He takes a hard line on campus disruptions, urban riots, law offenders, and social and political dissenters. He favors the use of force as the best way to cope with them. He is strongly patriotic and supportive of his government and of traditional political processes. He is opposed to some of the newer proposals in the economic welfare field, especially programs such as the guaranteed family allowance, which are designed to aid the really poor and minority groups. He generally supports a strong military and a powerful U.S. presence in world affairs.

There is, of course, some validity in these stereotypes or prototypes. Something approaching the liberal prototype may even be common on some college campuses. It is more likely, however, that opinion distributions among the mass public will mirror the confusion and lack of consistency suggested among contemporary political leaders. Persons who support the extension of welfare state measures, such as increased governmental medical assistance, may not always support policies designed to promote racial integration. They may not always have strongly opposed the Vietnam involvement. A lack of trust in government may be found alongside opinions opposing governmental race policies as often as opposition to Vietnam involvement.

The analysis of V. O. Key, with respect to opinion interrelationships in the late 1950s, found that in the mass public distributions of domestic and foreign policy, opinions were not related to each other. Persons who were liberal on domestic welfare issues and those who held conservative positions on such issues were equally likely to be internationalists with respect to issues concerning U.S. involvement in world affairs.[7] One who favored increased governmental activity in providing jobs, schools, and government medical assistance was not disproportionately likely to favor foreign aid or the proposition of U.S. involvement in world affairs.

Using data from the 1968 SRC survey, let us now look at how opinion distributions in the various issue areas are related to each other among the general population. How do opinions on an issue such as the medical assistance proposition correspond to opinions in other issue areas? The task is to ascertain whether or not those who agree with the medical assistance proposition are likely to take common specific positions on other issues, whereas those who disagree with the proposition tend to take a common position on the other side of the other issues. Methodologically this entails cross-tabulating responses on one issue with several selected issues, which represent the other issue areas. In order to simplify this exercise, six policy questions, each of which represents a major issue area, are used. The specific items used are (1) the medical assistance proposition, (2) the government school integration issue, (3) the item asking what should be done in Vietnam, (4) how to handle urban riots, (5) approval of the use of demonstrations, and (6) extent to which government can be trusted to do what is right. The responses to the medical assistance item and to each of these items were cross-tabulated against each of the remaining five issues. These cross-tabulations provide an indication of the extent to which opinion distributions on these several representative issues tend to be related to each other. Summaries of the results of these cross-tabulations are presented in Tables 3.3, 3.4, and 3.5, below.

The issue cross-tabulations indicate the extent of association between pairs of issues by showing the extent to which variations in responses to one item corresponds to variations in responses to another question. Let us present a hypothetical example to make this exercise clear. Suppose we want to know whether or not opinions on a national health insurance program are related to opinions respecting government school integration efforts. Do people who favor a health insurance program also tend to favor school integration efforts? Let us hypothesize that on both of these items the population is split 50–50. If all of those who favored the health insurance program also favored the school integration effort, and all of those who opposed the health insurance proposition opposed the school integration effort, we would have a very strong, even a perfect, correspondence. Opinions would be highly related to each other. We would be able to predict a person's opinion on the race question by knowing his position on the health insurance issue. We could say that a liberal response to the health insurance issue corresponded to a liberal response on the school integration issue.

On the other hand, we might have a situation in which half or 50 percent of those who said "Yes" to the health insurance issue said "Yes" to the school integration item, while the other half said "No."

TABLE 3.3 Relationship between opinions on medical assistance question and other issue opinions, 1968[a]

Position on medical assistance	% Favoring school integration efforts	% For stronger action in Vietnam	% Leaning toward use of force in handling urban riots	% Opposing demonstrations	% Saying government can be trusted all or most of the time
Favor	55%	32%	27%	50%	62%
Oppose	29%	45%	37%	59%	61%

Source: Data from 1968 SRC survey.
[a] The reader can find the wording of the questions and the overall distributions in Chapter II.

TABLE 3.4 Relationships between opinions on school integration and Vietnam and other selected issue opinions, 1968[a]

Position on school integration	% Favoring government medical assistance	% For stronger action in Vietnam	% Leaning toward use of force in handling urban riots	% Opposing demonstrations	% Saying government can be trusted all or most of the time
For	74%	28%	19%	43%	71%
Against	49%	44%	40%	61%	56%

What to do now in Vietnam	% Favoring government medical assistance	% Favoring school integration efforts	% Leaning toward use of force in handling urban riots	% Opposing demonstrations	% Saying government can be trusted all or most of the time
Pull Out	72%	49%	26%	50%	54%
Stay But End Fighting	64%	51%	22%	48%	69%
Stronger Stand	54%	33%	39%	60%	61%

Source: Data from 1968 SRC survey.
[a] The reader can find the wording of the questions and the overall distributions in Chapter II.

TABLE 3.5 Relationship between governmental trust, government benefit, and other issue opinions, 1968

Position on government trust	% Favoring government medical assistance	% Favoring school integration efforts	% For stronger action in Vietnam	% Leaning toward use of force in handling urban riots	% Opposing demonstrations
All or Most	62%	49%	35%	23%	51%
Some or None	61%	35%	38%	40%	57%

Source: Data from 1968 SRC survey.

Among those who were negative on the health insurance proposition, likewise, half favored the school integration effort and half opposed it. In this situation, opinion distributions on the two issues are not related to each other. We could not predict one's opinion on the race issue from his opinion on the health insurance issue. One could not refer to a cross-issue liberal or conservative syndrome on the basis of these two issues. A liberal on the health insurance issue (one who favored it) would not be any more likely than the conservative on that issue to take the liberal position (favor government school integration efforts) on the race issue.

We turn first to the relationships between the 1968 medical assistance item and the other representative issues. The medical assistance issue serves as a representative indicator of opinions on traditional welfare state type issues. Opinions on that issue are related fairly strongly to other economic welfare issues in the 1968 survey. In 1968 the government medical assistance proposition received the roughly 2 to 1 margin of support which seems generally characteristic of traditional welfare state issues in the mid- and late 1960s. Economic welfare and industrial relations type issues, as we indicated previously, are the issues that have tended to give shape and substance to the patterns of political conflict, identification, and coalitions over the past several decades. Thus relationships between opinions on this issue and opinions on the newer issues such as race, Vietnam, and public order ought to provide some indication of how new issue conflicts fit in with the more established configurations of conflict and agreement.

Data reporting the cross-tabulations between the medical assistance issue and five other issues are reported in Table 3.3. The figures in the tables indicate what percentage of those who favored the medical assistance proposition and what percentage of those who opposed it took similar stands on the other issues. The greater the difference in the percentage scores, the greater the relationship between the two opinions. The closer the percentages the less strong the association. For example, with respect to the governmental trust item the figures in Table 3.3 are extremely close—62 percent and 61 percent. These figures indicate that there is no relationship. Those favoring and those opposing the medical assistance proposition report trusting the government in almost identical proportions.

The data indicate a moderately strong relationship between opinions on the medical assistance issue and support for government intervention to integrate the schools. Those who favor the medical assistance proposition are more likely to support the integration efforts. A similar relationship was found between the medical assistance issue and support for the black job equality proposition. These findings are not presented in the table.

There is a relationship of a somewhat smaller magnitude between support for government medical assistance and proscriptions for action in Vietnam. Those who oppose the medical assistance proposition are slightly more likely to support taking stronger action than are those who favor it. The supporters of medical assistance are more likely than those opposed to favor the middle option calling for staying but trying to end the conflict. They are only very slightly more likely to endorse immediate withdrawal. On the item asking whether or not the respondent thought the involvement in Vietnam was a mistake the relationship is even less strong, though it is in the same direction. Those who favor the medical assistance proposition are slightly more likely to hold that the involvement was a mistake.

For the other three items the relationships are very weak. In the case of the governmental trust item, as we suggested above, the relationship is nonexistent. Those who favor the medical assistance proposition are slightly less likely to lean toward favoring the use of force in the handling of urban riots and less likely to oppose demonstrations.

These data suggest that the distributions of opinions on the medical assistance item are related significantly only to the race relations items. Liberals on the welfare state item are also somewhat more likely to take the liberal position in favor of government intervention with respect to race relations. The relationships between the more traditional medical assistance item and the other newer type issues are at the most only weak. Opinions on urban riots, demonstrations, and governmental trust and benefits seem to be held independently of position on the medical assistance issue. Opinions on the newer issues seem to divide the population differently from the more traditional economic welfare issues.

Of the various types of issue opinions it is race relations outlooks, especially the school integration and black job equality items, that are most closely related to other opinion distributions. We noted above that school integration is the issue for which opinions are most closely related to the medical assistance preferences. The data in Table 3.4 report that opinions on the school integration issue are weakly to moderately related to each of the other opinion distributions as well. Each of these relationships is stronger than those found with respect to the medical assistance proposition, with the exception of that between school integration and medical assistance. The two strongest relationships are with the medical assistance issue and the urban riots question. The correspondence between racial items and the urban riots question reflects the popular image of urban riots as primarily racial disturbances of one type or another. Consequently, the same attitudes and feelings that are brought to bear on race-relations issues are likely to influence outlooks on urban riots. Those who support the school integration proposition are less likely than those who oppose it to support stronger action in Vietnam and to oppose demonstrations. It is particularly interesting to note that those who oppose government intervention in behalf of school integration are more likely to indicate a lack of trust in government than are those who support the proposition. The same relationship holds with respect to the government benefit item. Those who are negative about government civil rights efforts are the ones who are most likely to say that the government works for the benefit of only a few big interests. These relationships run counter to the stereotype of the liberal presented above, which pictured the liberal who supported increased government efforts toward racial justice as the person most likely to be disenchanted with governmental action or lack of action.

Data at the bottom of Table 3.4 reports on relationships between the what to do in Vietnam item and the other issues. Because there are three responses to the Vietnam item these relationships are more difficult to discern. For the most part, it is those favoring a stronger stand in Vietnam that differ most from the other respondents. They tend to take more conservative positions on the other items, with the exception of the governmental trust item, which does not have clear conservative-liberal dimensions. Those favoring escalation are less likely to favor the medical assistance proposition, much less likely to favor school integration efforts, more likely to favor force for handling urban riots, and more likely to oppose demonstrations. This pattern fits the popular picture of opinion interrelationships. These relationships are strongest with respect to racial-type issues.

Those favoring pulling out immediately, on the other hand, do not differ systematically from those favoring a policy of staying but bringing the fighting to an end, the middle position. Despite the popular stereotype, the extreme doves are not consistently more liberal than those taking the middle position on most of the other issues. They are more likely to favor the medical assistance proposition. On the school integration issue, the use of force in handling urban riots item, and opposition to demonstrations question, however, those favoring a pullout have opinion distributions very similar to those favoring the middle position. On each of these three items, in fact, the slight differences that do occur between those two categories find those endorsing a rapid pullout slightly less likely to favor school integration and more likely to support force and to oppose demonstrations. With respect to the governmental trust item there is yet another pattern. The highest level of trust is indicated by those who took the middle position on the Vietnam item. The lowest level of trust was from those who favored a rapid pull out, with those supporting a stronger stand falling in between.

One additional set of relationships merits discussion. Those are the relationships between governmental trust and other policy opinions. In the preceding chapter we suggested that an issue of some importance today is the extent to which people feel the government can be trusted and that it is responsive. We indicated that over the past decade there has been a fairly substantial movement in the direction of more negative attitudes toward government. In response to specific survey items more people have come to say that the government cannot be trusted all or most of the time and that government works for the benefit of a few big interests rather than for all of the people. In order to understand this growing disaffection it is important to ascertain what, if any, types of issues this growing disaffection is associated with.

Data reporting on relationships between the item on governmental trust and five issues are presented in Table 3.5. The findings indicate that responses to governmental trust are most closely related to the school integration item and to the question dealing with urban riots.

The relationships with respect to these items are fairly strong. They differ from the popular image of political disaffection concentrated among the liberals and the radicals. Those who report feeling that the government can be trusted only some or none of the time are disproportionately likely to oppose school integration efforts and to favor the use of force in handling urban riots. These findings indicate that dissaffection is most strongly associated with opposition to civil rights and racial equality efforts, the conservatives on race relations issues rather than the liberals.

With respect to the other three policy issues there are virtually no relationships in evidence. Those reporting trust and those reporting a lack of trust are equally likely to take the liberal position on the medical assistance item. They are equally likely to support stronger action in Vietnam and to oppose demonstrations.

Let us return to the more general question of the extent to which there are within the population at large general configurations of policy preferences which cut across various issues areas. The data we have been looking at suggest that broad cross-issue coalitions of opinions exist only to a limited degree. The liberal and conservative prototypes suggested above do not hold for the public as a whole. The liberal on social welfare issues is somewhat more likely to be on the liberal side of race and civil rights issues. However, many who favor extensive government activity with respect to areas such as medical assistance and economic regulation do not support government intervention in behalf of school integration and black job equality. Fifty-five percent of those who favored the medical assistance proposal favored government efforts to integrate the schools, but 39 percent of the same promedical assistance respondents opposed school integration efforts. Those who favored the medical assistance item were only slightly more likely than those who opposed it to say that the Vietnam involvement had been a mistake.

Opinions on the more traditional welfare state issues do not relate very strongly or very systematically with opinions on most of the newer type issues. Welfare state type liberals do not always take what might be referred to as the liberal position on issues pertaining to race, Vietnam, and public order. There is a greater tendency toward greater interissue congruence among those at the conservative end of the issue spectrums, in comparison with the liberal end. Social welfare conservatives are more likely to be concentrated on the conservative side of other issues than are social welfare liberals to take liberal positions on the other type issues. For example, social welfare liberals are greatly split over support for racial integration policies. Social welfare conservatives, on the other hand, were opposed to school integration and black job equality measures by margins of better than 2 to 1.

To say that the extent of opinion interrelationships is not particularly strong and consistent is not to say that there are no patterns of interrelationship evident in the data. Rather, it is to say that there are a great many exceptions from the consistent liberal and the consistent conservative prototypes outlined above. One cannot predict with any great probability the position a person will take on one issue by knowing his position on another issue. When we take position on economic welfare issues as a base point and run it against other issues, there seem to be three broad issue groupings within the population, rather than the simple liberal-conservative dichotomy. For example, the cross-tabulation of the medical assistance issue against the school integration issue yields the following issue groupings: First, there are those who responded favorably to the medical assistance issue and supported school integration, the *consistent liberals*, with 33 percent of the respondents. Second, there are those who favored the medical assistance proposition but opposed the school integration proposal, the *welfare liberal-civil rights conservative*, with 24 percent of the respondents. Third, 21 percent of the respondents opposed both the medical assistance item and the school integration proposal, the *consistent conservatives.* Only 9 percent of the respondents opposed the medical assistance proposal but favored the school integration proposition. The patterns are not as clear when the medical assistance issue is cross-tabulated with other newer type issues, but the same general tendency is indicated. Persons who are liberal on the social economic issue, but take the more conservative position on the race issue, constitute nearly a quarter of the respondents.

The lack of strong issue interrelationships, especially at a period when there are a number of salient political issues, has important consequences for the organization of contemporary American political life. It is an important component of the present political disarray and confusion. The existence of several salient issue areas in which opinions are not strongly and systematically related to each other contributes to the difficulty that political leaders, political parties, and other political groups currently have in relating to and organizing political concerns and pressures. They make the formation and holding together of broad stable coalitions, based either on social groupings or common issue outlooks, very difficult. A labor union may find its members in strong agreement on economic and welfare policies, but split down the middle when it comes to race policies and support for the Vietnam involvement. Each of these issues may be very salient to large segments of the membership. A middle-class peace group may find its members in unanimous agreement concerning immediate withdrawal from Vietnam, but they may be widely divided when it comes to school integration or to the use of demonstrations to express political outlooks. As shall be made clearer in the following chapters, the newer issue not only do not relate to the traditional social economic issues, nor to each other very strongly; they also tend to cut through most of the significant social, demographic, and political groupings in different patterns.

The lack of strong and systematic interissue congruence is not a new phenomenon in American politics. As we pointed out earlier, V. O. Key, in his analysis of opinion interrelationship in the 1950s, found no association between opinions on domestic welfare issues and opinions on international involvement. Welfare liberals and welfare conservatives were equally likely to be internationalists and isolationists. In explaining how electoral coalitions, party loyalties, and other political groupings endured in the face of this lack of issue congruence, Key emphasized the relative saliency of different issues. He argued that for most of the electorate, domestic issues were the most salient issues and most likely to motivate electoral preferences and behavior. He reported that in 1956, 47 percent of the respondents to the SRC survey mentioned domestic concerns, whereas 16 percent mentioned foreign policy issues when they made references to the merits and demerits of the parties and candidates.[8] It was this greater concern with domestic welfare issues that tended to hold together the various political groupings. As long as domestic welfare issues were of primary concern to the welfare liberals, the fact that the liberals were divided about foreign policy issues was not particularly troublesome. The partisan and electoral coalitions that had formed around the New Deal issues tended to hold together as long as those economic welfare issues that had originally tied them together remained the most prominent political concerns.

The lack of interissue congruence at the present time is more critical as far as the formation and holding together of broad stable electoral groupings are concerned. Currently there is not any one dominant issue or issue area that is continuously salient for broad segments of the electorate. The traditional economic welfare issues no longer have overwhelming predominance. Race, Vietnam, public order, concern over the economy, and a number of lesser issues have vied for center stage on the contemporary political agenda. The relative saliency of these several issues seems to vary from time to time and from group to group. The coalition of voters built around one issue does not stay together when one of the other issues becomes the central focus. The shift in issue concern from the more traditional economic welfare issues to the newer issues has served to put the traditional coalitions in disarray. The lack of any one predominant issue area and the lack of strong systematic opinion interrelations have made it difficult for new broad stable coalitions to be formed.

Notes

[1] V. O. Key, Jr., *Public Opinion and American Democracy* (New York: Knopf, 1963), pp. 32–33.

[2] Ibid.

[3] The South, of course, was a major exception to this pattern. From the earliest days race and the issue of race relations have been central to political life in the South.

[4] Everett Carll Ladd, Jr., *American Political Parties* (New York: Norton, 1970), pp. 1–11.

[5] Richard Scammon and Ben Wattenberg, *The Real Majority* (New York: Coward-McCann, 1970).

[6] *Gallup Opinion Index*, Report Number 71, May 1971.

[7] Key, op. cit., p. 158.

[8] Ibid., pp. 172–173.

CHAPTER 4
POLITICAL OPINIONS AND
SOCIAL-ECONOMIC POSITION

Conflict between youth and adults over Vietnam; differences between southerners and northerners on racial desegregation; animosities between blacks and whites over racial justice and equality; disagreements between the middle class and the poor over welfare benefits; clashes between students and "hard hats" over war opposition and campus disorder—these suggest the popular images of political divisions in contemporary American society. Concepts such as "generation gap" and "racial polarization" have been added to more traditional notions such as class conflict and sectionalism to identify the structure of current political conflict.

In the preceding chapters we discussed the simple distributions of opinions in key issue areas. We pointed out the areas of consensus and conflict, stressed shifts in issue importance, and showed how opinions in different issue areas relate to each other. In this and the following chapters we explore the structure of issue conflicts and consensus. To what extent are opinions on various issues structured by occupation, age, geography, and race? Do conflicts tend to follow occupational lines, or do they cut across them? Do businessmen and professionals tend to assess U.S. involvement in Vietnam differently from manual workers? Are blacks more or less likely than whites to support social welfare measures? Or do opinions on welfare issues divide both blacks and whites similarly? Are young people more likely to endorse programs encouraging racial equality than are older people?

An understanding of political conflict requires knowing more than the extent of division and agreement within the population and the relative importance of various issues. It is also important to know what conditions structure patterns of conflict and consensus. In this chapter we investigate the relationship between social-economic position and opinions. In Chapter 5 we look at the role played by geography, race, and age in structuring contemporary opinion distributions.

Relationships between opinions on a given issue or set of issues and a social-economic condition, such as occupation, may follow several basic patterns. The possibilities lie on a continuum ranging from no relationship to a perfect correspondence. For example, let us suppose that public opinion is equally divided on the question of a proposed national health insurance program run by the federal government. That is, 50 percent of the people favor the proposition and 50 percent oppose it. Let us further suppose that we are interested in the extent to which one's opinion on the health insurance issue is related to his occupation, or the occupation of the head of his household. To simplify the issue let us divide occupational position into two general categories: white-collar occupations (professional, businessmen, clerical and sales workers) and manual workers. At one extreme we could have a distribution structured like that in Table 4.1. In this situation all of the white-collar workers are opposed to the health insurance proposition, and all of the manual workers are in favor of it. Opinions on health insurance are very strongly related to occupational position. There is wide disagreement within the population on the issue, but total agreement within these broad occupational groupings. Occupation can be said to structure the conflict or disagreement on the health insurance issue. The conflict follows and does not cut across occupational lines.

At the opposite extreme the pattern would look like that in Table 4.2. In this instance there is no relationship between occupational position and opinion on the health insurance proposition. The white-collar workers and the manual workers are both divided 50–50 on the issue, exactly the same as the entire population. There is conflict, but the differences are not at all structured by these occupational categories. Division on the health insurance issue cuts across the occupational groupings.

TABLE 4.1

Occupation	Position on health insurance	
	FOR	AGAINST
White collar	0%	100%
Manual worker	100%	0%
Total population	50%	50%

TABLE 4.2

Occupation	Position on health insurance	
	FOR	AGAINST
White collar	50%	50%
Manual worker	50%	50%
Total population	50%	50%

Another pattern of responses which lies in between the extremes would indicate a still different relationship. One might have a distribution like that in Table 4.3. In this situation there is some relationship between occupational position and opinion, but it is only of moderate strength. White-collar workers are somewhat more likely to oppose the proposition, and manual workers to support it. The conflict is structured somewhat by occupation, but it also cuts across occupational lines to a considerable extent.

If opinion distributions on a variety of issues are structured similar to that in Table 4.1, or in a pattern falling between Table 4.1 and Table 4.3, one could say that political conflict is structured according to occupational lines. On the other hand, if opinion distributions tend to be structured more similarly to those in Table 4.2, or lie in between Table 4.2 and Table 4.3, one would say that occupation does not play a very important role in structuring political conflict.

Political and social theorists have emphasized the impact of social-economic position (occupation, income, social class identification, social status, etc.) in determining political attitudes and behavior. One of the most commonly accepted propositions about the politics of industrial societies is that political conflicts tend to follow economic and social class divisions. Although this interpretation is associated with the Marxist tradition, other approaches to social and political analysis

TABLE 4.3

Occupation	Position on health insurance	
	FOR	AGAINST
White collar	40%	60%
Manual worker	60%	40%
Total population	50%	50%

also have emphasized social-economic factors in explaining variations in political outlooks and behavior.

In this chapter we seek to answer three questions. First, has social-economic position become more or less important in structuring political opinions and outlooks in American society over the past few decades? Second, to what extent are opinion distributions in different issue areas associated to different degrees with social-economic position in the contemporary period? Third, do opinions on the newer type issues—race, Vietnam, public order, and governmental trust—tend to be more or less closely related to social-economic divisions than are opinions on more traditional issues?

Although the important role of social-economic conditions in determining political interests and conflicts has been accepted with respect to industrial societies in general, there have been some qualifications with regard to how important social-economic divisions have been in American society. The most common interpretation is that social class and related factors have played a less significant role in structuring political life in American society than in most other advanced industrial nations, though not necessarily an unimportant one. Furthermore, it seems evident that economic divisions became more important during the twentieth century, especially following the restructuring of political life that resulted from the Great Depression, the enactment of New Deal legislation, and the development of the Roosevelt coalition in the 1930s. Among the major changes in political life that occurred during the 1930s was the shift of political orientations, especially voting behavior, party identification, and attitudes toward economic and welfare policies, to follow more closely occupational and economic divisions. Economic welfare and industrial relations issues emerged as the most important focus of political attention and conflict.

Seymour Lipset and Robert Alford, two sociologists who have focused on the class basis of voting in the United States and other Western nations, have noted the correspondence between class and party vote over the last few decades.[1] Both of them indicate that class voting in the United States has increased during the twentieth century and suggest that it is likely to continue to increase in the future. Alford makes this prediction very explicit in the final section of *Party and*

Society. His argument is based on two assumptions. First, Alford holds that politics and political conflict in industrial society center primarily around differences between economic groupings over the distribution of resources in the society.[2] Lipset in a similar vein argues that the partisan electoral struggle is basically "a democratic translation of the class struggle."[3] The second assumption made by Alford is that in the United States several nonclass factors have been influential in determining voting and party loyalties. He notes regionalism, religious-ethnic ties, and traditional loyalties or attachments as factors that have counteracted the impact of class in American politics. Regionalism, religious-ethnic ties, and traditional loyalties, he maintains, are being eroded. They are losing their political influence in modern society. As the potency of these factors diminishes, Alford predicts, voting and partisan conflict will become more class-oriented.[4]

Contrary to Alford and Lipset, we assert that over the past few decades there has been a decrease in the extent to which social-economic position has structured political differences and that issue conflict in the contemporary period is likely to be less associated with economic divisions than it was in the 1930s, 1940s, and 1950s. More in keeping with Lane, we suggest that conditions related to class or social-economic position are less likely to serve as sources of political conflict or potential conflict today and in the immediate future than two or three decades ago. Even on issues that have been closely associated with economic interests such as welfare and industrial relations policies we anticipate a weakening of the association between opinion and social-economic position. The newer political concerns would seem even less likely to be closely associated with economic divisions.

Several different measures or indices of social-economic position are used in the identification of social-economic differences. In this analysis we employ the occupation of the head of the household as the major indicator of one's position in social-economic strata. Some attention is also given to family income. Occupation and income are widely used measures in public opinion and political analysis. Data on them have been obtained in most public opinion and political surveys with at least some consistency over time. Students of social class and social-economic status generally regard occupation as the best single indicator of a person's position in the social-economic hierarchy.[5]

Since occupation is the primary factor in the analysis of this chapter, and the key concern is with ascertaining whether or not there are differences in political outlooks between people in different occupational groupings, let us make clear just what occupational categories we use and how the population is distributed among the various occupational groupings. The occupation breakdown used in this analysis is based on eight general categories: (1) professional and technical workers, (2) businessmen and managers, (3) clerical and sales workers, (4) skilled workers or craftsmen and foremen, (5) unskilled workers or operators, (6) service workers, (7) laborers, and (8) farmers. Respondents that did not fall in one of these eight categories are not included in this analysis.

In our analysis we refer to an occupational hierarchy or the ordering of occupations along a status or prestige continuum. In this ordering the professional and technical workers are at the top, followed by businessmen and managers and clerical and sales workers in that order. These three groupings are often placed together to constitute a nonmanual workers category in analysis in which a simple manual and nonmanual workers distinction is used. Continuing on down the occupational hierarchy are the skilled workers, unskilled workers, service workers, and laborers, in that order. These make up the manual category. When the notion of occupational rankings is used, the farmers are omitted. They do not fit systematically into the industrial occupational stratification rankings. Consequently, when we develop measures of the level of association between occupation and political opinions, the farmers are not included in the calculations.

In most of the data presentations of this chapter we employ six occupational categories. This reduced number is obtained by putting the unskilled workers, the service workers, and laborers together in a common category called the nonskilled workers. This makes two major groupings of manual workers: the skilled and the nonskilled. Opinion distributions for the farmers are generally presented at the end of the occupational groupings to remind the reader that they do not fit into the industrial occupational hierarchy.

In Table 4.4. we indicate the proportion of workers which fall into each of these eight occupational categories so that the reader can get a better idea of the relative size and the magnitude of the groupings when we talk about the skilled workers, the farmers, professional and technical workers, and the like. In order to suggest the changes in the occupational structure over the past few decades percentages of workers falling in the several occupational categories for 1950, 1960, and 1970 are included in Table 4.4. The two most significant shifts are the increased proportion falling in the professional and technical category and the large decrease in the farmer category. Between 1950 and 1970 the professional and technical category increased from 7.5 percent to 14.2 percent. The farmers decreased from 12.4 percent to 4.0 percent. The twenty-year period saw a fairly substantial shift toward the nonmanual occupations—those at the higher end of the occupational heirarchy. In 1950, 37.5 percent fell in the three nonmanual occupations. In 1970, 48.3 percent fell in the three categories at the top. The percentage of skilled workers remained constant. Those in the nonskilled category decreased slightly.

Using measures of occupation and of income we attempt to see the extent to which persons in different occupational categories and with different incomes tend to take different positions on political issues.[5] How extensive are the differences in various issue areas? What are the directions of these relationships—which groups tend to be more liberal and which more conservative on different types of issues? How stable have these relationships been over time? We turn first to the question of change over time in the structuring of opinion differences

TABLE 4.4   Relative distribution of work force in major occupational categories 1950, 1960, and 1970

	1950	1960	1970
Professional and Technical	7.5%	11.2%	14.2%
Managers, Officials, Proprietors	10.8	10.6	10.5
Clerical and Sales	19.2	21.3	23.6
Craftsmen and Foremen (Skilled)	12.9	12.8	12.9
Operatives	21.2	18.0	17.7
Nonfarm Laborers	5.9	5.5	4.7
Service	11.0	12.5	12.4
Farmworkers	12.4	8.1	4.0

Source: Computed from data in *Statistical Abstract of the United States 1971* (92nd ed.) Washington, D.C., 1971, p. 222.

and then to an investigation of the relationship between occupation and income groupings and political opinions in the contemporary period.

The issue area in which one would anticipate the greatest correspondence between social-economic position and opinions or preferences is economic welfare and industrial relations policies. We already have suggested that these issues were particularly salient political concerns during the 1930s and the immediate post–World War II era. They are the issues around which political contests centered and over which the political parties tended to divide. It is precisely on these types of issues that both individual and class interests and concerns are likely to be most pronounced and divisions most apparent. Historical-political analysis has indicated that the several economic and political factors that occurred in the 1930s did lead to partisan support and issue positions that tended to follow occupational and income lines. Persons in higher-status, nonmanual occupations were more likely to oppose government welfare programs and the extension of economic and industrial regulation than were lower-status manual workers. The higher the income level the more likely the person was to oppose these types of governmental activities. In his *Public Opinion and American Democracy*, using data taken primarily from the 1956 SRC survey, V. O. Key found that occupation tended to structure policy opinions more than any of the other factors that he looked at. With respect to most economic welfare and industrial relations issues, Key found an ordered pattern of increased support as one moved down the occupational hierarchy, from professionals and businessmen, to clerical-sales workers, to skilled workers, to unskilled workers and laborers.[6]

In order to investigate the question of whether or not the extent of these relationships between occupation and income and opinions on economic welfare type issues has changed over the past few decades, we obtained data from Gallup, Roper, and NORC surveys going back to 1936. We were able to find a series of generally comparable questions in three important policy areas that had been asked periodically from 1936 through the mid-1960s. These questions have to do with (1) the extent of government regulation of business, (2) the level of welfare spending, and (3) the question of whether a program of government medical insurance should be adopted. We obtained nine questions asking about government regulation of business, running from 1936 through 1966; eight questions pertaining to the level of welfare spending, running from 1936 through 1964; and ten questions pertaining to government health assistance programs, running from 1943 through 1962.[7]

In order to assess the amount of correspondence between opinions on these issues and occupation and income we computed two measures of association between the distribution of opinions and distributions along an occupational and an income continuum. In this manner we sought to see the extent to which differences in occupation and income tended to be associated with differences in opinions on government regulation of business, welfare spending, and government health programs. Measures of association were computed for each of the 27 individual questions. The two measures of association used are the gamma coefficient (a standard statistic for measuring the association between two ordinal variables) and a range of difference score.[8] The range score was computed by finding the difference in the percentage of the highest occupational and income categories and those in the lowest categories who indicated a liberal response[9]—that is, those who favored more government regulation of business, more spending for welfare, and supported some sort of government health program. Thus, if 70 percent of the manual workers favored increasing the amount of government regulation of business, while only 30 percent of the business and professional persons took that position, we would substract the 30 percent from the 70 percent for a range of difference score of 40. With respect to both the gamma coefficient and the range of difference measure, higher scores indicate a stronger relationship. Thus, a range score of 40 would indicate that opinions on government regulation of business are fairly highly structured by occupation.

For purposes of analysis the time span from 1936 to the present was divided into three periods. The first period (Period I) runs from 1936 through 1945. This goes from the middle of the Great Depression and the time at which the New Deal and the New Deal coalition were being formed through the end of World War II. It was a period of great change, particularly with respect to the role of government in the economy. We anticipated that during this period there would be a fairly strong relationship between social-economic position and opinions on welfare and industrial relations issues. The second period (Period II) runs from 1946 through the 1950s. This was a time of adjustment to, consolidation of, and occasionally reaction against, the changes that had taken place during the preceding decade. There continued to be some controversy, especially during the first part of this period, over welfare state measures: whether they should be extended, kept the same, or reduced. This was also the period of transition to the period of postwar affluence that Lane and Galbraith argue had developed by the mid or late 1950s. We had anticipated that social-economic position would remain strong in ordering opinions, but that the relationships would be less strong than during the first period. The third period (Period III) runs from 1960 to the present. This includes the period of economic affluence, the emergence of consensus in support of welfare state measures, as well as the development of new conflicts in the late 1960s. We anticipated for this period the dampening of economic and industrial conflict and expected that opinions on welfare state type issues would be less strongly associated with differences in economic position. In short, we anticipated that as we moved from Period I through Period II to Period III the correspondence between social-economic position and opinions would decrease. That is, the gamma coefficients and the range of differences scores would become smaller over time.

The results of this analysis are presented in summary form in Table 4.5. Rather than present the gamma coefficients and range of differences scores for each of the questions, a mean was computed of the scores for the survey responses falling within each of the three periods. These summary scores suggest a substantial decrease over time in the extent of association between occupation and income and opinion differences for each of these three issues. The drop is from a rather strong relationship to almost no relationship. Note that most of the change occurs between Period II and Period III. There is relatively little decrease between Periods I and II.

In interpreting these trends an additional factor should be kept in mind. The changes toward less association over time between opinions and income and occupation do not necessarily result from any movement toward overall agreement on the questions asked. For the most part the overall population remains somewhat divided in its

TABLE 4.5 Changes over time in the level of association between opinions on three welfare-industrial relations issues and occupations and income

| | Government regulation of business | | | | Level of welfare spending | | | | Government medical program | | | |
| | OCCUPATION | | INCOME | | OCCUPATION | | INCOME | | OCCUPATION | | INCOME | |
	Gamma[a]	Range[b]	Gamma	Range	Gamma	Range	Gamma	Range	Gamma	Range	Gamma	Range
Period I 1936–1945	.39	28	.36	30	.34	25	.47	35	.32	22	.36	25
Period II 1946–1959	.32	25	.35	41	.30	23	.32	36	.35	23	.36	25
Period III 1960 on	.07	7	.11	12	.12	7	.19	12	.23	12	.14	12

Source: Data from a series of Gallup, Roper, and National Opinion Research Center national surveys, running from the late 1930s through the mid-1960s. Data obtained from the Roper Public Opinion Research Center.

[a] The gamma scores reported here are means computed by averaging the gamma scores obtained for several comparable items within each of the specific time periods. See Appendix B for a brief discussion of the gamma coefficient.

[b] The range scores reported here are the means of the range of difference scores computed for a series of comparable items within the specified time period. The range of difference score was obtained by subtracting the percentage of persons in higher occupations and income levels who gave a liberal answer to the item from those in the lower occupations and income groupings who gave liberal answers.

responses to specific questions. The significant change indicated here is
that in the 1930s, 1940s, and early 1950s the divisions of opinion tend
to follow, rather closely, divisions in occupation and income position.
In the 1960s, though the same amount of overall division might be
evident, that division is not as structured by differences in occupation
and income level as it tended to be earlier. Data presented in Figure 4.1
make this point clearer and show more vividly the type of change that
has taken place in the structuring of responses to these items over the
past few decades. The bar graphs represent responses to two questions
about government regulation of business. The top display shows the
percentage of persons in various occupational categories responding
that they would like to have less government regulation of business in
response to a Gallup poll question posed in October 1940. The bottom
display shows the patterning of respondents who replied that government regulation of business is too strict in response to a January 1966
Gallup poll question.

Both of the questions provided three response categories. In both
1940 and 1966 the respondents were divided, though there was a shift
over time in the direction of acceptance of the existing level of
regulation. In 1940 somewhat over half of the respondents fell in the
"less regulation" category, with the other half fairly evenly split

1940: Percent preferring less government
regulation of business

1966: Percent saying that government
regulation of business was too strict

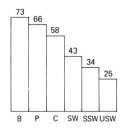

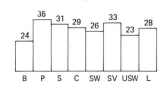

Key: B = Business   C = Clerical   SW = Skilled Workers   SV = Service
        P = Professionals   S = Sales   USW = Unskilled Workers   L = Laborers

Data from American Institute of Public
Opinion, Study No. 219 (Oct. 1940).

Data from American Institute of Public
Opinion, Study No. 723 (Jan. 1966).

FIGURE 4.1.   Responses to two questions about government regulation of
business in 1940 and 1966

between those wanting more and those wanting the same amount. In 1966 somewhat less than half of the respondents replied that they thought government regulation of business was about right. The remaining half was evenly divided between the other two categories. For our purposes the significant factor is the change in the extent to which occupation orders the responses. In 1940 there were significant differences between occupation categories in the percentage of persons saying that they wanted less government regulation of business. As one moves from the bottom to the top of the occupational status ladder there is an orderly and incremental increase in the percentage of respondents saying that there should be less regulation. The increase from unskilled workers to businessmen is 48 percentage points. In the responses to the 1966 item differences between occupational groupings are relatively small. In addition there is no systematic or orderly progression from one end of the occupation hierarchy to the other. The range of difference between the businessmen, on the one hand, and the unskilled workers and laborers combined, on the other hand (a range in occupations that is roughly comparable to the range between unskilled workers and businessmen in 1940), is only 1 percentage point, compared to the 48 points in 1940.

These trend data suggest that socioeconomic conditions, such as occupation and income, have become less important in structuring opinion differences on economic welfare and industrial relations issues during the 1960s. The change, at least in the issues mentioned above, is considerable, and has important consequences for the structure and tone of contemporary political life. Let us now look at the relationship between opinions and socioeconomic conditions in the contemporary period. Opinion distributions for a variety of issue items in the late 1960s were presented in Chapter 2. To what extent are the distributions on these various issues related to, or structured by, occupation and income? What is the general across-the-board relationship over all of these issue areas? What is the relative association between social-economic position and opinions in different types of issue areas? The data in Table 4.5 show changes between the 1960s and earlier years. What has been the direction of change, if any, over the past decade?

Figure 4.2 presents data showing the relative proportion of respondents in six occupational categories taking a "liberal" position on

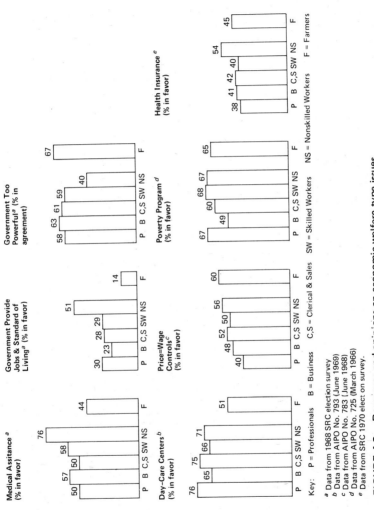

FIGURE 4.2. Responses and opinions on economic welfare type issues

Key: P = Professionals   B = Business   C,S = Clerical & Sales   SW = Skilled Workers   NS = Nonskilled Workers   F = Farmers

[a] Data from 1968 SRC election survey
[b] Data from AIPO No. 793 (June 1969)
[c] Data from AIPO No. 783 (June 1968)
[d] Data from AIPO No. 725 (March 1966)
[e] Data from SRC 1970 elect on survey.

seven welfare state issues. The three bar graphs at the top represent three items from the 1968 SRC survey. One item has to do with the government helping people get medical assistance at low cost. Another has to do with the government seeing that everyone has a job and a good standard of living. The third item does not deal directly with a specific policy. However, the question of the role and power of the federal government has been a central focus in the welfare state controversies in the United States. Opinions on this issue tend to correspond closely with opinions on other social welfare policies, and not so closely with other types of issues. The data are presented in bar graphs so that the similarities and differences between occupations will be easily seen.

The data from these three items indicate that occupation continues to structure opinions on these issues, but only to a limited extent. Those in the lowest-status occupation grouping, the nonskilled workers (a category composed of semiskilled laborers, domestic household workers, unskilled factory workers, and the like), are more likely to take liberal positions on these issues than are the others. The structuring of opinion by the occupational hierarchy is different in two important respects from what it was in earlier decades. First, the range of difference between professionals, managers, and businessmen, on the one hand, and manual workers, on the other hand, is not as great as in earlier years. On the whole, the level of association between occupation and opinions on welfare state issues seems to have been higher in the decades preceding the 1960s than over the past few years. Second, the significant increase in liberal responses comes between the skilled and the nonskilled workers, not between the manual workers and non-manual workers. In each of these three opinion distributions the frequency of positive responses of the skilled workers is very close to those of the professionals, businessmen, and clerical and sales workers. It is less similar to that of nonskilled workers. The change in the position of the skilled workers, relative to professional-business people, on the one hand, and nonskilled workers, on the other hand, can be seen more clearly from a comparison of data from the 1968 and the 1956 SRC surveys. The same question concerning government medical assistance was asked in both surveys. The frequencies of positive responses for these three occupation groupings in 1956 and 1968 are as follows:

	1956	1968
% of professional-businessmen giving positive responses	45%	54%
% of skilled workers giving positive responses	61	58
% of semiskilled, servicemen and unskilled workers giving positive responses	67	75
Range of difference between professional-business and skilled workers	16	4
Range of difference between skilled workers and nonskilled workers	6	17

These comparative data suggest an important shift in the pattern with which occupation structures opinions on welfare-type issues. Comparable questions with respect to the job and standard of living issue and the government "too powerful" item were not asked in the 1950s. In 1968, however, the skilled workers are even closer to the professional and business people and further from the nonskilled workers on those two issues than on the medical assistance question.

The four bar graphs at the bottom of Figure 4.2 portray the relationships between occupation and four more specific economic welfare-industrial relations issues that have been of concern over the past few years. These include support for day-care centers, support for price-wage controls, attitudes toward the poverty program, and attitudes toward a national health insurance program. The bar graphs suggest that opinions on these issues are even less strongly associated with differences in occupation than were the three items from the 1968 SRC survey.

With respect to issues in the foreign policy area, the patterns are different for different types of issues. With respect to the more traditional issues of foreign aid and isolationism, occupation continues to order opinion preferences. Those in higher-status occupations are more likely to support foreign aid and less likely to agree with the isolationist position than those in lower-status occupation. This has been the general pattern of relationship during the post–World War II period. V. O. Key found this same relationship with respect to a series of indicators of internationalism, using data from the early and mid-1950s. Commenting on the response patterns to various items, Key says: "Whatever the form of the question, the professional and business classes ordinarily include the fewest outright isolationists. The proportions disposed toward withdrawal from the rest of the world are commonly highest among unskilled laborers and farmers, although these contrasts are far more marked on some issues than on others."[10] As the bar graphs in Figure 4.3 indicate, relationships between occupation level and positions on foreign aid and isolationism follow an orderly, incremental pattern. For the most part, with each step up the industrial occupation hierarchy there is increasing support for foreign aid and opposition to the withdrawal proposition.

The shift over time in the level of association between occupation and policy preferences that was evident with respect to economic welfare-industrial relations issues does not appear with regard to these traditional international affairs positions. The level of association between social-economic position and opinion on these issues appears to have remained the same, and maybe even to have increased slightly over the past decade or two.

In contrast to the more traditional foreign policy issues, opinions

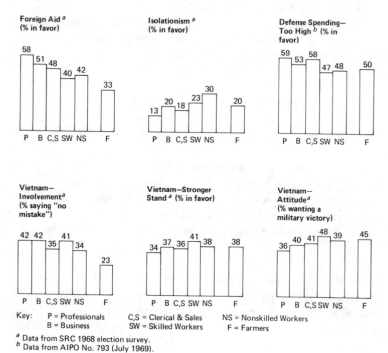

Key: P = Professionals   C,S = Clerical & Sales   NS = Nonskilled Workers
     B = Business   SW = Skilled Workers   F = Farmers

[a] Data from SRC 1968 election survey.
[b] Data from AIPO No. 793 (July 1969).

FIGURE 4.3.   Occupation vs. foreign policy and Vietnam opinions

and evaluations concerning the involvement in Vietnam appear to be unrelated to occupation. The data presented in the bar graphs at the bottom of Figure 4.3 indicate that the distributions of opinions among persons in different occupation categories are generally similar to each other. This salient issue, that so intensely divided the American population, divided each of the occupational groupings as well. Conflict over Vietnam cuts across the occupational and income divisions, rather than being structured by them. The opinion division within the sample, with roughly 36 percent saying the involvement was not a mistake and 62 percent that it was, is mirrored in each occupation grouping. Only the farmers look substantially different. None of the response distributions within the major occupations differs more than a few percentage points from the national distribution in response to the item asking what we should do in Vietnam.

Vietnam has been an issue of great controversy, but a conflict that has not been structured by social-economic position. [11] In Chapter 2 it was noted that there was considerable change between 1964 and 1970 with respect to evaluations of the Vietnam involvement and opinions regarding what type of future action should be taken. Basically the change was a shift from a strong majority in support of the involvement to a good margin reporting opposition. The same change took place within each of the major occupation groupings. This was not a situation in which persons in one occupation category tended to be on one side and those in other categories on the other side with a movement toward convergence over time. Professionals, managers, salesmen, plumbers, truck drivers, and janitors all tended to shift in the same direction at the same time.

There is one additional distribution represented in Figure 4.3. This has to do with opinions regarding the level of defense spending. In a July 1969 Gallup poll, respondents were asked whether they felt too little, too much, or the right amount of money was being spent for defense. The data represented are the percentages in various occupations responding that too much was being spent for defense. Professional, business, and clerical and sales persons are slightly more likely to choose the "too much" response, but the differences between them and manual workers and farmers are relatively slight. Occupation is not very important in structuring the division of opinion on this issue.

A second major area of conflict in the contemporary period is in the

area of race relations. As we suggested in Chapter 2, questions
pertaining to race have become extremely salient issues over the past
decade. The race question involves a number of particular issues over
which the population is very much divided. To what extent are
opinions on race issues structured by occupation? The relationships
between occupation and opinions on three different race-related
questions are presented in Figure 4.4. The bar graphs across the top of
the figure suggest that occupation does structure opinions on the three
race items, to some extent. The pattern, however, is different from that
found with respect to either the social welfare or the foreign affairs
issues. With respect to the school integration and the black jobs
propositions, the nonskilled manual workers are the most supportive of
government action in behalf of equality and integration. The second
most supportive are the professionals, at the opposite end of the
occupational hierarchy. Businessmen, clerical-sales workers, skilled
workers, and farmers fall in between. Roughly the same pattern is
evident on the question pertaining to the speed with which civil rights
groups are pushing racial change. The professionals and those in the
nonskilled manual labor categories are the least likely to say "too fast."
With respect to the school integration item and the speed of change
item, the skilled workers are among the least supportive of integration
and most negative about the efforts of civil rights proponents. Less than
a third support the school integration proposition.

As was the case with economic welfare issues, it is the nonskilled
manual workers who look the most dissimilar from the other occupational groupings. They appear more supportive of racial integration and
civil rights efforts. It is possible that this higher level of support might
result, in part, from the higher proportions of blacks among the
lower-status occupations. On the one hand, blacks are decidedly more
supportive of government efforts directed toward racial integration and
racial equality. At the same time, blacks are concentrated disproportionately in the less prestigious occupations, especially service workers
and unskilled laborers. One might anticipate, therefore, that the
overrepresentation of blacks among the nonskilled manual workers
might account for some of the differences between the nonskilled
workers and other occupational groupings. The bar graphs at the
bottom of Figure 4.4 represent the occupational distributions for the

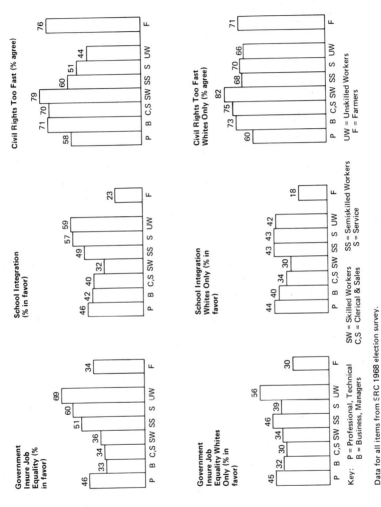

FIGURE 4.4. Occupation and race relations opinions

Data for all items from SRC 1968 election survey.

Key: P = Professional, Technical   SW = Skilled Workers   SS = Semiskilled Workers
      B = Business, Managers   C,S = Clerical & Sales   S = Service
      UW = Unskilled Workers
      F = Farmers

same three items among whites only. With the blacks removed the nonskilled manual workers are not as different from the other occupational groupings as they were with the blacks included. Without the blacks, support among the service workers and the unskilled laborers for the job equality and school integration propositions drops substantially. The drop among the other occupational categories, those in which blacks tend to be underrepresented, is very slight. The skilled workers, however, continue to be less supportive of racial integration and equality than the nonskilled workers, even when only the white population is taken into account.

The two other issue areas with which we have been concerned also represent problem areas that have become salient over the past decade. These are public order and attitudes toward government. Bar graphs relating the distributions of opinions within occupation groupings for three public order items and three items concerning feelings about the government are presented in Figure 4.5. On the whole, opinions on these items are not strongly associated with differences in occupation. The levels of association are quite low. There are, however, several nuances that merit note.

In regard to the three items indicating feelings of governmental trustworthiness and responsiveness, skilled workers and farmers stand out as least likely to express positive feelings. For example, in response to the question of whether the government works for the benefit of all of the people or a few big interests, the percentage of skilled workers replying that it works for the benefit of all is 43 percent, 12 percentage points below the occupational grouping with the next lowest support, not considering the farmers. The same pattern holds with regard to the other two items. Although the differences are not of great magnitude, the pattern is consistent. These findings suggest where in the population feelings of discontent or potential political disaffection seem to be most prevalent.

On the public order issues slightly different patterns are evident. In each of the distributions the figures represent hard line, get tough responses to various activities perceived as threats to public order and safety. The professionals are consistently the least likely to support the hard line position. The farmers are the most likely to favor getting tough. Between these polls, the different issues yield different orderings. After the farmers, it is the skilled workers who are most

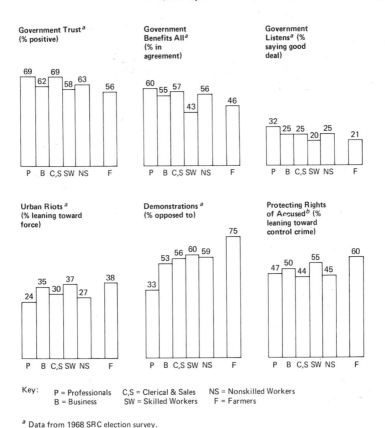

Key: P = Professionals   C,S = Clerical & Sales   NS = Nonskilled Workers
      B = Business   SW = Skilled Workers   F = Farmers

[a] Data from 1968 SRC election survey.
[b] Data from 1970 SRC election survey.

FIGURE 4.5.   Occupation vs. governmental trust and public order opinions

likely to endorse the hard line position. The widest occupational differences are found in response to the item asking about the use of demonstrations that have the approval of local officials. In regard to this item the range of difference between professionals and the farmers is 45 percentage points. All of the other occupational groupings are clustered fairly close together. While only one-third of the professionals express outright disapproval, and three-fourths of the farmers do, disapproval is expressed by between 53 and 59 percent of those in the other four occupational categories.

Taking into consideration the whole range of issues, it seems that occupation position plays only a limited role in structuring the distributions of opinions on policy issues in the current period. Whether one considers an issue over which there has been considerable conflict and close division, such as involvement in Vietnam and desegregation of the schools, or an issue upon which there is general consensus, such as the medical assistance proposition and rejection of isolationism, there are no instances in which persons at one end of the occupational hierarchy are strongly lined up on one side of the issue and those at the other end are massed on the other side of the issue. There are no instances in which issue conflict is structured by differences in social-economic position in a pattern approaching that of Table 4.1, above.

Having made this assertion, let us quickly point out that there continue to be opinion distributions and issue areas where preferences are related to occupational differences. It is not that occupation, or social economic position, has altogether ceased to play a part in structuring or determining political opinions, but, rather, that the level of association between occupation and opinion is not as strong as it was during earlier decades. In addition, the patterns with which occupation structures opinions on many issues do not always follow the more traditional mode of a manual worker-nonmanual dichotomy, or one in which an incremental movement up or down the occupation ladder is associated with incremental and linear variations in opinions or preferences.

There continues to be some relationship between occupation and opinions on economic welfare issues. The most pronounced differences, however, are between nonskilled workers on the one hand, and all of the other industrial occupations, including skilled manual workers, on the other hand. The nonskilled workers are the most likely to take the liberal position on these issues. The skilled workers, on the other hand, are not skewed toward the liberal side any more than are the non-manual professional, business, and clerical-sales respondents.

The issue area in which opinion differences follow most closely the model of incremental changes in opinion distribution with each step up or down the occupation ladder is the traditional foreign policy area. The general overall level of association between occupation and opinion

is highest with respect to the isolationism item. It is also relatively high with respect to the foreign aid question. The higher the occupational status the more likely one is to support foreign aid and to reject the isolationist proposition.

Two occupational groupings deserve more extensive comment here. These are the skilled workers and the farmers. For the most part we have omitted the farmers from systematic discussion in the foregoing analysis. This is because farmers do not fit into the general occupational stratification system of industrial society in any systematic way. They are omitted from the computation of statistical measures of association and from the discussion of how opinions are distributed according to an occupational ladder or scale. Skilled workers merit additional comment because they stood out in distinctive ways in some of the distributions discussed above, and because they so seldom fell where traditional notions of relationships between occupations and political preferences would anticipate.

We noted above that with respect to social welfare type issues the skilled workers, more often than not, exhibited opinion distributions very similar to the nonmanual workers and dissimilar from their fellow manual workers. With respect to some items, in fact, the skilled workers appear as the most conservative of occupational groupings, even on some economic welfare type issues. With respect to the race relations and civil rights issues the skilled workers are generally the least likely to endorse programs designed to promote racial equality or integration. This pattern is especially evident with respect to school integration and the speed with which civil rights are being pushed. Data from the 1968 SRC survey also report that among the industrial occupational groupings the skilled workers are least likely to endorse the principle of integration, to support equal accommodations, and to believe that blacks should be allowed to live anywhere they want. On the Vietnam items the skilled workers do not look very different from the other occupational groups. They are only slightly more likely to support the hawkish or hard-line position. Excluding the farmers, the skilled workers are the most likely to endorse the use of force as the most appropriate response to urban riots and to support doing all that is necessary to stop crime as the major objective in the prosecution of accused criminals. With respect to both of these items, it is interesting

to note, the skilled workers look very similar to the business-managers. They are the most dissimilar from the nonskilled manual workers and the professional, both of whom show more interest in protecting the rights of the accused. On the three items dealing with governmental trust and responsiveness, the skilled workers consistently have the highest incidence of negative attitudes.

Taken together, these findings offer some support for the recent tendency to view the skilled worker—the construction worker, the plumber, the carpenter, the toolmaker, the railroad engineer, the automobile mechanic, the television repairman, and the like—as "conservative" in the context of contemporary political issues and attitudes. These people are not, at the present time, the strong proponents of expanding programs and services in the area of economic welfare and industrial relations. In regard to the race issue the skilled worker is the most likely to resist changes in the position of blacks. He seems to be among the most reluctant to support and accept social and economic change.

The comparatively negative attitudes among the skilled workers regarding the government, along with their more negative feelings about change in race relations and tendency to take a hard line on public order issues, suggest strong feelings of discontent with the current thrust of government policy, as he views it. The skilled worker tends to see the government supporting or engaging in programs and actions designed to aid the blacks and the very poor. Rightly or wrongly, he often perceives these efforts as operating at his expense rather than for his benefit. He sees the sons and daughters of the privileged engaging in riots, demonstrations, and other behavior generally considered immoral or illegal, for which they receive little or no punishment. He sees the young flouting the values of hard work, patriotism, and respect for law and authority, which he was taught must be abided by and believed in for acceptance and success. He sees a government that seems responsive, not to his interests and needs, but instead to those of others, many of whom he sees as less deserving. These are the types of discontent which Wallace sought to exploit in the 1968 election and again in the 1972 Democratic primaries.

The farmers, a small and still-dwindling proportion of the population, exhibit opinion distributions similar to those of the skilled workers. They seem to share many of the same negative attitudes and

outlooks, often more so. On the economic welfare and industrial relations issues the farmers are decidedly more likely to oppose both new and existing activities than are any of the other occupation groupings. For example, the government medical assistance proposition was endorsed by 62 percent of the entire sample in 1968. Only 44 percent of the farmers favored it. There seems to have been a movement toward comparatively greater opposition to welfare state type measures among farmers over the past two decades. V. O. Key reports on the basis of 1956 data that farmers ranked second among the occupation categories in their level of support for the same medical assistance proposition. Their level of support was only slightly behind that of unskilled workers and well ahead of the general sample in 1956. [12] In regard to race relations the farmers are less likely than almost any of the other occupation groupings to support civil rights efforts of the government and changes in the status of blacks.

In the area of nondomestic issues the farmers are the least likely to support foreign aid. They tended to be more opposed to the Vietnam involvement and to the general conduct of the war. The farmers are more inclined toward the use of force in dealing with urban riots and decidedly less likely to sanction demonstrations than are any other occupation group. On the governmental trust and responsiveness issues, the farmers are distributed in patterns similar to those of the skilled workers, exhibiting comparatively high levels of distrust.

The opinion distributions of the farmers are the most deviant from the general distributions on political attitudes and policies. They appear to be the most out of tune with the contemporary thrust of government policies and actions and to exhibit the highest levels of dissatisfaction and disaffection concerning contemporary politics. This condition, of course, is not surprising for a group that now constitutes a very small proportion of the population, and during a time in which the rhetoric of political and social concerns are focused on the urban areas and their problems.

Occupation is, of course, only one indicator of social-economic position. Levels of family income and education are two other indicators often used in he measurement and analysis of social-economic position. Data on family income and on the level of education obtained by the respondent were included in most of the surveys used in this analysis. In order to obtain a more complete picture of the relationship between social-economic position and political opinions, correlation coefficients were computed between the major policy issues from the 1968 survey and both income and educational background. The overall results were very similar to those found between occupation of head of family and political opinions, which were discussed above. Since the results are so similar, there is no need for extensive discussion of them here. The correlation coefficients indicating the level of association between income and opinions on seventeen issues are presented at the right side of Table 4.6. These figures allow one to see rather clearly both the overall levels of association of 1968 and the relative levels of association between the several different issue areas.

TABLE 4.6 Relationship between income and political opinions: 1960, 1964, and 1968

Issue area	1960[a]	1964	1968
Government Medical Assistance	.33	.30	.21
Government Job Guarantee[b]	.22	.24	.13
Federal Aid to Education[b]	.16	.13	.06
Federal Government Too Powerful	*	.18	.11
Government Black Job Guarantee	.16	.13	.04
School Integration	.01	.05	.03
Civil Rights Pushed Too Fast	*	*	.01
U.S. Isolation	.36	*	.36
Foreign Aid	.12	.13	.20
What Do Now in Vietnam	*	.18	.08
Attitude on Vietnam	*	*	.05
Mistake to Get Involved in Vietnam	*	.25	.16
How Respond to Urban Riots	*	*	.04
Approve of Demonstrations	*	*	.17
Government Benefit All or Few	*	.10	.02
Trust Government to Do Right	*	.07	.07
Government Listen?	*		.10

Source: Data from SRC surveys, 1960, 1964, 1968.

[a] The measure of association reported here is the gamma coefficient. See Appendix B for a brief discussion of this measure. The same trends over time are ascertained when Kendall's tau and Pearson correlations are computed.

[b] The wording of the 1960 question is quite different from that of the 1964 and 1968 question, though the issue area is the same; thus, the 1960 responses and those in 1964 and 1968 cannot be very accurately compared.

*No even roughly similar question asked in that particular survey.

A major proposition of this chapter has been that the extent to which political opinions are structured by, or related to, differences in social-economic position is less strong today than it was in earlier decades. Earlier in this chapter we reported, and discussed, some trend data that demonstrated the relative weakening of the impact of occupation and income in structuring opinions on three welfare state-industrial relations issues. At that point we were drawing comparisons between the 1960s and the three previous decades. We also want to know if the trend indicated by those data has continued through the past decade. To what extent has there been any trend in the level of association from 1960 on? In order to investigate this issue we computed correlations between income and several issues taken from the 1960 and 1964 surveys that are fairly comparable to some of those items from the 1968 study. Comparable items for all three studies were obtainable for three welfare state issues, two race relations items, and one of the traditional foreign policy questions. Items from the early 1960s were not available to tap relationships on some of the newer type issues. The coefficients for the several items are presented in Table 4.6, alongside those computed for the 1968 questions. These data suggest that with respect to the welfare state type issues the level of association between income and opinion has continued to decline through the 1960s. This is demonstrated best by the medical assistance items. For these questions the format has been consistent over time. Here the gamma coefficients drop from .33 in 1960, to .30 in 1964, to .21 in 1968. This change in the level of association has occurred while the level of support for the proposition has remained fairly constant. The same decrease in level of association between income and opinion is evident with respect to the job guarantee and "aid to education" items. The 1960 questions for these two items, however, are somewhat different and elicit very different levels of support. With respect to both of these issues, however, the major decrease in association with income occurs between 1964 and 1968 when the questions were the same. A similar decrease is apparent in the level of association with respect to the black job guarantee question. There is no change over time with respect to the school integration item. The same nonrelationship is apparent for each of the three years.

On the two more traditional, international relations questions the level of association is higher than for the other items, and at least with respect to the foreign aid question the trend is toward a higher rather than a lower level of association. It should be recalled that it was with respect to these two items that the highest level of association was found with occupation and political opinion in the discussion above.

The data in Table 4.6 offer additional support for the preceding discussion and analysis. Social-economic position is relatively unimportant in the structuring of political opinions at the present time. With respect to several salient political issues there is considerable conflict and disagreement. For the most part, however, that disagreement does not follow occupation or economic lines. The trend evident between the 1960s and the preceding decades appears to have continued through the 1960s. There are variations between the different issue areas. Although the relationships between opinions and social-economic position are weaker in the late 1960s than in the earlier years with respect to welfare state type issues, relationships in this area remain higher than the other issue areas, with the exception of the traditional foreign affairs issues. In regard to most of the newer type issues, those issues that have developed as salient political concerns and as major focal points for political conflict only over the past few years, the level of relationship between opinion distributions and level of income and occupational status is particularly small.

Notes

[1] Seymour Martin Lipset, *Political Man* (Garden City, N.Y.: Doubleday, 1960), pp. 303–331; and Robert R. Alford, *Party and Society* (Chicago Rand McNally, 1963), pp. 225–231.

[2] Alford, op. cit., pp. 326–336.

[3] Lipset, op. cit. pp. 230–278.

[4] Alford, loc. cit.

[5] For most of the data analysis here the respondent's designation of the occupation of the head of the household is used to establish the respondent's occupation category.

[6] V. O. Key, Jr., *Public Opinion and American Democracy* (New York: Knopf, 1961, pp. 123–130.

[7] These data were obtained through the Roper Public Opinion Research Center, International Survey Library Association.

[8] For a discussion of this measure of association see Appendix B in the present book.

[9] Alford, op. cit., pp. 73–79.

[10] Key, op. cit., p. 131.

[11] For a report on other research that came up with this conclusion, see Sidney Verba et al., "Public Opinion and the War in Vietnam," *American Political Science Review*, LXI (June 1967), pp. 317–333.

[12] Key, op. cit. p. 126.

CHAPTER 5
REGION, RACE, AGE

Social-economic position is not the only source, or potential source, of political conflict in modern societies. As we suggested in the preceding chapter, geographic region and religious-ethnic association often have been important in structuring political attachments and opinions in the United States. In some instances the following of regional or ethnic lines has led to opinion distributions that cut across social-economic divisions. For example, in much of the South since the end of the Civil War white citizens in all occupational categories have tended to be Democrats for reasons having to do with regional identifications and animosities that stemmed from the conflict between the North and the South. The prevalence of issue conflicts based on social divisions other than class or economic lines was one reason why political conflict during the early part of American history was not very strongly associated with social-economic divisions.

In the past decade political and social commentators have emphasized the role of race and age in determining and structuring political and social outlooks. On the one hand, there has been talk about increasing racial polarization, the tendency for whites and nonwhites to hold contrary preferences and opinions and to view each other with hostility. On the other hand, the notion of the generation gap has become very popular. This notion asserts that young people, usually defined as those under thirty, tend to have political and social perspectives that differ from those of people over thirty years of age.

In this chapter we investigate the extent to which region, race, and age tend to structure political opinions in the contemporary period. In previous chapters we have noted that there are a number of issues over which the public is fairly widely split; some of these constitute intense conflict. With respect to most of these issues, as was suggested in the preceding chapter, the differences of opinion do not seem to be very closely associated with differences in occupation, income, or education —factors that tended to structure conflict over economic welfare and industrial relations issues over the past few decades. Here, we wish to explore the extent to which differences of opinion at the present time are related to other potential sources of political and social cleavage. Do opinions regarding racial equality and integration tend to follow geographic lines? Has the conflict over the Vietnam involvement, which seemed to be little related to social-economic position, tended to follow age and racial lines? To what extent are there differences in political outlooks among different age and racial groupings?

GEOGRAPHIC REGIONS

Sectionalism has been an important component of American political life and rhetoric. Throughout much of American history, political conflict has been viewed popularly, though maybe not always accurately, as centering around differences in outlook and interest among several geographic regions. Even as the Constitution was being written, conflicts between the North and South arose over tariff and trade provisions and over some aspects of slavery. The South, because of its agrarian economy, was interested in policies making it easy to sell its agricultural goods abroad and to import manufactured goods from Europe in exchange. Significant economic interests in the North, on the other hand, were tied to the development of a strong industrial and commercial economy. Representatives of these interests preferred protective tariffs so that they could sell their products at home without interference from outside competition.

As the population expanded westward, conflicts of interest and, thus, political differences developed between the West and the East over the spending of public money for internal improvements (e.g., roads and communication links) and over economic policies determining the quantity and price of money. The common textbook interpretation of much of nineteenth-century politics has viewed political conflicts largely in terms of such regional differences. The South wanted free trade; the North, protective tariffs. The South supported and defended the institution of slavery; the North opposed it, especially its expansion into new areas. The West wanted cheap money for expansion and support of agriculture and mining operations and to ease the burden of economic debts, which this expansion often entailed. The East wanted to maintain the value of money in order to protect its investment and economic interests. The Midwest tended to be isolationist, preferring not to become involved in the affairs of the rest of the world. Easterners, on the other hand, because of their economic interests in trade and their geographic location closer to Europe, tended to favor international involvement. During the second half of the nineteenth century and well into the twentieth century national partisan conflict was strongly structured by regionalism. The Democrats received much of their strength in national elections from the overwhelmingly Democratic South. The Republican party relied on the Northeast as its major bastion of strength. The intensity of regional differences, and the level of conflict between the North and the South in the mid-nineteenth century are, of course, testified to by the Civil War. The impact of that conflict in terms of regional loyalties and animosities is still felt, more than a century later.

The habit of viewing political conflicts in terms of geographic regions is very much a part of American political outlook today. There is a tendency to talk about politics in terms of feelings, preferences, and reactions in the several geographic regions. Presidential tickets are put together with a mind toward balancing the candidates geographically—a northerner and a southerner, an easterner and a midwesterner, and so forth. Cabinets, and even the Supreme Court, are made up with some attention to geographic representation and balance. In a great many ways Americans look at politics as structured by regionalism, as if the geographic regions constituted units with different political interests and outlooks.

How relevant are such conceptions of regional structuring to an understanding of the distribution of political opinions today? To what extent do differences in opinions in the issue areas we have been considering tend to follow regional or geographic patterns? In order to investigate these questions we have cross-tabulated opinions on thirteen major policy issues from the 1968 SRC survey with the four major geographic regions. The four major sections generally referred to in the discussion and analysis of regions in the United States are used: the Northeast, the Midwest, the South, and the Far West. Bar graphs showing the relative distribution of opinions within the four major areas are presented in Figure 5.1.

The distributions presented in the figure offer little evidence that opinion differences are structured along regional lines. Rather, they suggest a considerable cross-regional uniformity on most issues. There are, of course, some variations—but the differences are small and, often, they do not follow popular conceptions. It is, for example, the people in the Midwest, not the South, who tend to be most conservative on welfare and economic issues. Easterners are slightly less likely to support a hard line on Vietnam. Southerners are least likely to countenance demonstrations, but differ only marginally from those in other regions on race issues. Even where these differences do take place, the amount of variation is rather small. Only on the school integration question and the issue pertaining to demonstrations and protests does the range of difference between any two regions reach as high as 15 percentage points. On none of these issues can one suggest that region structures political conflict, with those in one region leaning substantially in one direction and those in other regions leaning in the other direction. There may be other political and social values and preferences over which the populations of different regions show greater diversity, but on these major national issues the differences are slight.

Two areas in which this lack of regional difference holds deserve additional comment. The findings here are at variance with some popular assumptions. These have to do with comparisons between the South and other regions with respect to domestic welfare issues and opinions regarding race relations. Of all of the regions, it is the South that generally is thought to deviate most from national norms and from the other sections. This has been and continues to be true with respect to voting turnout and party loyalty. The South since the Civil War has been poorer and less industrialized than other parts of the nation.

The conventional wisdom, or popular understanding, corroborated by the votes of southern congressmen and pronouncements of southern political leaders has held that people in the South are more conservative than those in other areas of the nation with respect to domestic welfare issues. By and large, southern representatives to Congress have tended not to support new ventures in government social and economic intervention over the past few decades. From the later 1930s through the early 1960s southern Democrats, in conjunction with conservative Republicans, were primarily responsible for defeating bills providing for

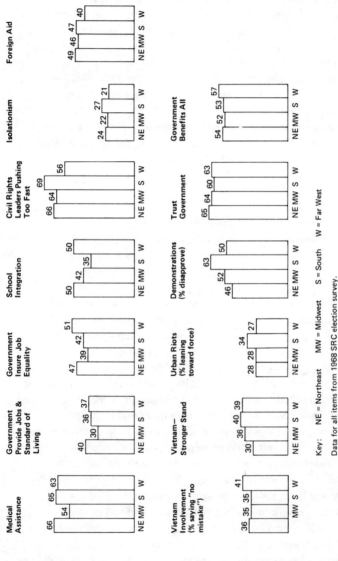

FIGURE 5.1. Geographic regions and opinions

Key: NE = Northeast   MW = Midwest   S = South   W = Far West

Data for all items from 1968 SRC election survey.

aid to education, urban renewal, medical assistance, and minimum wage increases. This has contributed to the widespread notion that political opinion distributions in the South are skewed to the conservative side. The opinion distributions in Figure 5.1, however, suggest that opinion distributions on economic welfare type issues are not more conservative than those in the remainder of the nation. On both the medical assistance and the job and standard of living guarantee, southerners appear equal to northeasterners in their level of support. It is those in the Midwest who tend to be somewhat more conservative.

V. O. Key, more than a decade ago, noted the same phenomena. There was, he reported, a discrepancy between the general conception of southern opinions and actual opinion distributions.[1] The explanation Key offered for this discrepancy between the votes and statements of southern leaders and the opinions of southerners, as reflected by national samples, seems relevant to our findings and discussion. Key pointed out that in the South participation in electoral politics has been considerably lower than in other parts of the nation for some time. By and large, the lower level of participation has meant very low voting rates among the lower social-economic groups, both black and white. Over the past few decades the poor and manual workers have been the ones most likely to support government welfare state type efforts. Southern political leaders and representatives, because of the low level of election participation of those not so well off, have been less likely to be influenced by low income and minority group welfare liberals than have their nonsouthern counterparts. By the same token, they have been beholden to the wealthier and more conservative people. More than in other sections of the country, political leaders and representatives have not very faithfully mirrored public opinion. These relationships are changing in the wake of increased electoral participation by lower-income southerners, and especially by southern blacks.

The relatively slight differences between opinions in the South and other regions with respect to race issues are more surprising and significant. They reflect more than a misleading popular notion. They suggest a shift in opinion structuring. In his public opinion analysis, based on the 1956 SRC data, Key reported that in the area of race relations, and only in that area, did the South stand out from the rest of the nation.[2] He found that southerners were considerably more likely to oppose government school desegregation efforts than were people in the rest of the nation. The 1968 data show less interregional difference, indicating that some shift has taken place. Those in the South tend to be more likely to support efforts of the federal government directed toward school integration; those in the North have become slightly less likely to support the proposition. These shifts reflect both a change in the meaning of school desegregation and a nationalization of the whole issue of interracial relationships. Shifts in the focus of civil rights concerns toward such questions as opportunities in jobs and housing and racial demonstrations and urban unrest have also tended to be nationwide in impact and thus to affect opinions and behavior outside of the South.

Data from two Gallup Polls indicate that a significant change has occurred in the South over the past decade in the acceptance of racially integrated schools. In 1963 and again in 1970 Gallup asked a national sample of whites the following question: "Would you, yourself, have any objections to sending your children to a school where a few of the children are Negroes? Where half are Negroes? Where more than half are Negroes?" [3] The responses to these questions, comparing North and South in 1963 and again in 1970, are presented in Figure 5.2. The trend data indicate a substantial movement toward greater acceptance of mixed schools among both white northerners and white southerners. However, the change has been much more pronounced among southerners. Between 1963 and 1970, for example, there was a drop of 45 percentage points in the proportion of white southerners who reported objecting to sending their children to schools in which there were a few blacks. In 1963 there was a considerable difference between whites in the South and those in the North on this issue. In 1970 the difference between northerners and southerners was very small. The same trends are apparent with respect to schools that are half black and schools that are more than half black, though the magnitude of change is less. These data offer further evidence that opinions in the South, even on the race issue, which has contributed so much to the deviant character of southern political life, have become less distinct over the past few years. In interpreting these data, it should be kept in mind that the questions refer solely to the racial makeup of schools. They do not

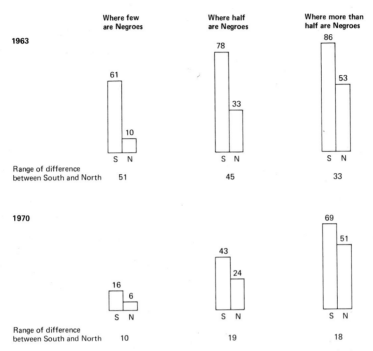

The question was asked of a sample of white parents only. "Would you, yourself, have any objection to sending your children to a school where a few of the children are Negroes? Where half are Negroes? Where more than half are Negroes?"

Data from *Gallup Opinion Index* No. 59 (May 1970).

FIGURE 5.2. Change in comparison of white parents' attitudes on school integration North vs. South, 1963 and 1970—percent of white parents objecting to sending their children to schools

reflect responses to government activities or programs designed to bring about racial integration or racial balance. Nor do they touch upon the issue of the use of bussing to bring about racial integration, an issue for which there is currently much opposition.

We have found little evidence to suggest the existence of significant regional structuring of political opinions or of political cleavages that follow sectional lines. With respect to opinions on the issues considered, opinion distributions within the various regions tend to be similar.

Where conflict exists it tends to cut across geographic regions. Even the South does not differ significantly from other regions on these general issues of national concern. This does not mean that there are no differences of opinion between regions. Opinion distributions in the South, for example, continue to differ from the rest of the nation with regard to some moral issues and behavioral patterns. Southerners, for example, are less likely to report that they drink alcoholic beverages and are more likely to support the prohibition of liquor than are people in other sections. Although the differences are becoming less pronounced than in the past, southerners are more likely to identify with the Democratic party and less likely to vote and to participate in electoral politics than are citizens in other regions. There continues to be a particular style and tone to southern politics, and in the relationship between the South and the rest of the nation, that is somewhat distinctive and that makes the South more responsive to such things as the Wallace movement in 1968 and the Goldwater candidacy in 1964.

Despite such differences the data indicate that the broad geographic regions do not structure opinion differences on contemporary national policy issues. The geographic or sectional cleavages which existed, or were presumed to exist, during early periods of American history are not apparent today. Nevertheless, American political discourse and perceptions continue to be influenced by notions of regional perspectives and loyalties—and this vocabulary will probably be with us for some time to come.

RACE

Over the past two decades race has become a very significant issue in American politics. Its influence has been felt in several different respects. We pointed out earlier that the race issue emerged during the decade of the 1960s as a salient political issue, one over which the population has been very deeply divided. Here we explore another aspect of the impact of race on contemporary American politics. To what extent do political opinions tend to follow racial lines? To what extent do whites and nonwhites exhibit opinion distributions that distinguish them from each other? What is the impact of racial division in determining the extent and structure of political conflict in the contemporary period?

In order to investigate the impact of race on the structuring of political opinions, we have cross-tabulated opinions on the policy issues with a white-black dichotomy for a series of contemporary issue items, most of which are taken from the 1968 SRC survey. The results are reported in Figure 5.3. Bar graphs are used to indicate visually the differences among the two racial groupings. The distribution for the entire sample is shown next to those of the racial groupings to show the relative impact of the racial groupings in determining the distributions within the entire population.

Even a very casual glance at the data represented in Figure 5.3 make it clear that blacks and whites tend to hold different opinions on most issues. More than the other potential cleavage structures we have looked at, race divides the population with respect to a great many issues. The differences between the distributions of opinions among blacks and whites are often quite extensive.

The two issue areas in which black and white opinions are most divergent are economic welfare and race relations. On the race issues (school integration and black job equality) blacks show almost unanimous support for government action. Ninety percent of the blacks in the sample favored federal government intervention in school integration. Eighty-nine percent supported government intervention in behalf of black job equality. Endorsement of these propositions among whites was less than a majority. The range of difference between blacks and whites was 53 percentage points on the school integration item and 51 percentage points for the black job proposition. Blacks by similarly high margins support the medical assistance proposition and the job and standard of living guarantee. In fact, the unity of black support is higher on the medical assistance item—94 percent in favor—than on any other item. Whereas the white respondents are quite reluctant to support the notion of government guarantee of job opportunities when coupled with providing for a good standard of living, blacks show a great willingness to endorse the proposition. On all of the social welfare type issues the blacks are decidedly more liberal than whites. They show little hesitation at having the federal government intervene in the society to provide for economic security and regulate social and economic relationships. They exhibit little fear about the power of the

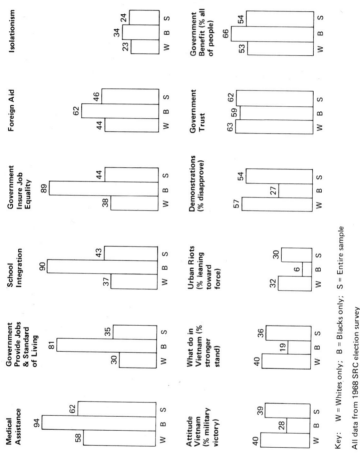

Key: W = Whites only; B = Blacks only; S = Entire sample

All data from 1968 SRC election survey

FIGURE 5.3. Race and issue opinions

federal government. On these types of issues, in particular, it can be said that opinions tend to follow racial lines. Issue conflicts tend to be structured, in part, by racial position. For the blacks, in particular, opinions on these issues cut across occupational lines. Regardless of their occupation, blacks tend to line up on the liberal side of race and welfare type issues. Among the whites as well, interoccupational differences on racial and welfare type issues are less pronounced when only white respondents are taken into consideration. Some of the greater tendency of those in lower-status occupations to be more supportive of welfare measures and government intervention in behalf of racial integration and equality, which was noted in the preceding chapter, results from the disproportionate-concentration of blacks among the lower-status occupations.

The large differences between blacks and whites, on social welfare and civil rights activities, the near unanimity of support for government intervention in these two areas among the blacks, and the tendency of blacks from all occupational groupings to take a similar position seem to have significant ideological implications. On the entire spectrum of such issues, including the item concerning the power of the federal government, blacks exhibit little tendency to fear, oppose, or mistrust the notion of federal government action and involvement. In this important respect, it seems that blacks stand outside that significant strand in American political and cultural values which stresses localism and states' rights and opposes the interference of the federal government. This strand has had an important impact throughout the course of American history and has influenced the political values and preferences of almost every social, political, and geographic group.

Although the differences between blacks and whites are most pronounced with respect to welfare state and race relations issues, they are not confined to those areas. Blacks in 1968 seemed to be somewhat more likely to oppose the involvement in Vietnam and were less likely to support hard-line proposals calling for escalation of the conflict and military victory. Blacks also are somewhat more likely to support foreign aid and to accept the isolationist position with respect to U.S. involvement in world affairs. As one might expect, since urban riots have generally been associated with racial tensions and conflict, the blacks are somewhat less likely to choose the hard-line position in dealing with such disturbances. They are also less likely to oppose demonstrations and protests. Whereas more than half of the white respondents in 1968 registered outright opposition to demonstrations, only slightly more than a quarter of the black respondents in 1968 took that position.

The issue area in which blacks and whites tend to be least divergent in their distributions of opinions pertains to the area of governmental trust and responsiveness. Blacks and whites trusted the government to do what is right in almost equal proportions in 1968. The blacks were considerably more likely to support the contention that the government works for the benefit of all of the people rather than just a few big interests. These findings may be surprising, given the general climate of race relations during the middle and late 1960s with the growing militancy of black political protest and the many instances of riots and protests involving blacks. However, it should be kept in mind that during the half a decade prior to the time these questions were asked some very important advancements were made in national civil rights legislation, most notably the Civil Rights Act of 1964 and the voting rights legislation of 1965. In addition, the early and mid-1960s had seen the enactment of important legislative programs that were designed to be of benefit to the poor, many of whom were black. The poverty program, Medicare, rent subsidies, and the federal aid to education provisions are among the most significant programs in this respect. Moreover, it is not unimportant that during the preceding eight years two Democratic presidents had been in the White House, both of whom had strongly espoused the causes of racial equality and integration while serving as president. As we pointed out in the last chapter, the two occupational groupings most apt to express negative evaluations of the government with respect to the issues of governmental trust and responsiveness were the skilled workers and the farmers. These are also the two occupational groups that were least likely to favor government action to promote racial equality and integration. Negative feelings about the government in 1968 seemed to be most closely associated with racial feelings, with those most opposed to civil rights efforts expressing the most negative feelings toward government.

The extent to which these indicators of public disaffection from government are related to which party controls the presidency, and the feelings people have regarding the particular actions and commitments of that administration, are indicated by the changes in black and white responses to the governmental trust and responsiveness items between the 1968 and 1970 surveys. In 1968 Johnson, a Democrat, was concluding his tenure in the White House. At the time of the 1970 survey, Nixon, a Republican, who had acquired a rather negative image among blacks and black leaders, had been president for a year and a half. Data showing changes between 1968 and 1970 among both blacks and whites with respect to governmental trust and responsiveness are presented in Table 5.1. As we noted in Chapter 2, there was a decrease in the proportion of respondents giving positive evaluations of governmental responsiveness and trust between 1968 and 1970. The data in Table 5.1 point out that though both blacks and whites moved in the negative direction, the shift among blacks was significantly greater than that among whites. In 1968 the blacks were more likely to say that the government worked for the benefit of all. In 1970 the relative positions of blacks and whites had reversed. The whites showed a decrease of 6 percentage points in the proportion responding that the government works for the benefit of all the people. Among the blacks the drop was 32 percentage points. On the governmental trust issue, the white drop-off was 7 percentage points, while black opinion shifted 19 points. It is also interesting to note that among the skilled workers—those who were among the most negative on these two items in 1968—there was very little change between 1968 and 1970. In fact, there was a slight increase of 2 percentage points in the proportion of

TABLE 5.1 Changes 1968–1970 in governmental trust and who benefits from government among blacks and other groups

	Trust government all or most of the time		Government benefits all of people	
	1968	1970	1968	1970
Blacks	59%	40%	66%	34%
Whites	63	56	52	46
Skilled Workers	58	56	43	45
Entire Sample	63	55	55	45

Source: Data from the 1968 and 1970 SRC surveys.

those saying that the government works for the benefit of all.

In the current period there are significant differences among blacks and whites over nearly every area of public policy concern. Differences in political outlooks seem to be more highly associated with racial differences than with any other potential structure. These variations are also very pronounced with respect to partisan attachment and voting behavior. In responses to the 1968 SRC question on party identification 87 percent of the blacks identified themselves as Democrats, whereas only 41 percent of the whites chose that position. Among those reporting that they voted for president in 1968, 97 percent of the blacks reported having voted for the Democratic candidate, whereas 36 percent of the whites reported having voted for Humphrey. As with opinions on the race and welfare state type issues, the near solidarity of preference among blacks and the tendency of partisan preferences to cut across economic divisions testify to the saliency of race in determining the political outlooks of blacks.

The differences in policy preferences and partisan attachments between blacks and whites are not a new development. They seem to exist as far back as public opinion data allow one to make comparisons. The differences may have become more pronounced in the last decade. More important, the political significance and consequences of these differences have altered drastically over the past decade. First, the whole concept of race and racial divisions has become a part of the national political consciousness. There has also been an increase in black voting participation and a tendency for blacks to organize and to pressure in behalf of their own interests, values, and policy preferences. A dissident minority that has become politicized, that has developed modes and channels of political expression, and that is disposed to push its interests and preferences makes for a very different ball game from one in which that minority is passive, lacking in political consciousness, and does not have channels for political expression and pressure. The latter was the situation among blacks until the past few years.

There is one additional component of the implications of the structuring of political conflict along racial lines that needs to be mentioned here. That is the great discrepancy in size between the black and white populations. Blacks constitute only about 10 percent of the American population. They made up 10 percent of the 1968 SRC sample. This means that even when the opinions of blacks are skewed far over to one side of an issue, they have little impact on overall opinion distributions. The relatively slight effect they have on overall opinion distributions can be readily appreciated by looking at the third bar in the various bar grams in Figure 5.3. For each issue there is a bar representing the distributions of black opinion, white opinion, and the distribution for the entire sample. The comparative distributions for the two subgroups and the sample with respect to the medical assistance item and the school integration item illustrate the situation very well. Fifty-eight percent of the whites approve of the government medical assistance proposition. A whopping 94 percent of the blacks approve of it. When the blacks and whites (along with others) are considered together, the percentage approving is 62. The almost unanimous endorsement of the blacks only increases the approval within the whole sample by 4 percentage points. The same pattern is apparent on the school integration issue. Black approval is 90 percent, 51 percentage points higher than among the whites. When blacks are added to the whites, the increase in approval rises only 6 percentage points, from 37 to 43 percent.

The situation of polarization of opinions between two segments of the population when one of these segments is a very small, and distinct, minority presents some important problems for the resolution of certain issues in American society. Without strong allies among the majority groupings it is difficult for the minority to exercise much influence or to achieve its will through the normal electoral and legislative processes. On an issue such as the medical assistance proposition, it does not make too much difference. Although the opinion distributions are far apart, there is a majority in favor among both blacks and whites. The proportion of blacks is simply much higher than that of whites. On race-related issues, in which the blacks have a particularly crucial stake, the situation is certainly more difficult. With the blacks increasingly conscious of their own interests and policy preferences on the one side, and a majority of whites on the other side, and with whites on some types of issues becoming more concerned and resistant to change, we have the seeds of disruption of the normal policy-making channels or the creation of large-scale frustration and resentment on the part of the minority. This, of course, is what has been happening in many areas of race relations in the past few years. Issues such as forced bussing to ensure racial integration in the public schools, and racial quotas in hiring procedures, are issues that in the past few years have been particularly apt to lead to this sort of problem. We return to this problem in Chapter 7 in which we discuss the problems of the parties and electoral system in responding to these new areas of conflict.

AGE

Age constitutes another dimension or structure according to which political opinions and political cleavages might be structured. The past few years have witnessed the popularization of a notion concerning the distrubution of opinion differences according to age. This is the assumption that the youth tend to have somewhat distinctive political values, preferences, and outlooks that distinguish them from older population groupings. The term applied to this interpretation is "generation gap." The proposition that youth are likely to have political interests and grievances that separate them from their elders has been espoused by at least one theorist of social stratification. In his book *Power and Privilege*, Lenski argues that in advanced industrial societies conflict between age groups, particularly between youth and older people, is likely to emerge as an important and difficult source of social division and conflict.[4] Seeming to anticipate the content and tone of the youth rebellion and demands of the late 1960s, Lenski argues that advanced industrial societies tend to keep young people in positions of training and preparation for adult roles for increasingly long periods of times. Youths are consequently deprived of many of the powers and privileges of adulthood until relatively late in their lives. This deprivation, he contends, may lead to the creation of common grievances concerning control over, and participation in, the making of institutional, economical, and political decisions that affect their lives. Coupled with this situation, Lenski continues, is a tendency for youths to spend more of their time in situations in which they are congregated together among their own age cohorts with only limited contact with, and influence from, persons other than fellow youths. The former condition, Lenski maintains, provides the basis of common grievances and the latter the setting for the development of a group consciousness and consequently the rise of an "age class" that sees itself at odds with other "age classes."

In order to investigate whether or not a generation gap (defined as a tendency for differences in opinions to follow age lines) exists with respect to major policy issues in the current period, we divided the 1968 SRC sample respondents into three age groupings. Accepting the popular determination of 30 as the age that separates the younger from the older generation, we designated those under 30 as one category. Inasmuch as the national surveys have been concerned with voting, and until recently the right to vote in most states has begun at 21, the youngest grouping contains primarily persons from 21 through 29. The rest of the sample was divided into two groupings. The three age categories used are (1) those under 30; (2) those 30–49 years of age; and (3) those 50 and over. As was the case with race, region, and occupation, opinions on a series of major contemporary political issues were cross-tabulated with these age groupings. The results of these relationships are presented in bar graph form in Figure 5.4.

Two factors stand out in the data presented in the figure. First, there are only slight tendencies for differences in opinion to be structured by the age groupings. Second, where differences do exist, the gap is more often between those over 50 and the rest of the population, rather than between those under 30 and their elders, as the generation gap notion would predict. On most of the issues, those under 30 and those 30 to 49 exhibit similar opinion distributions.

There is very little variation between age groupings on the medical assistance and the job and standard of living issues. The oldest grouping is slightly more supportive of the medical assistance proposition. This probably reflects the fact that the operating Medicare program applies specifically to older people. On the race issues those over 50 are least supportive of civil rights and racial integration, with differences most pronounced on the school integration issue. Those in the oldest category are most likely to support the isolationist proposition and to oppose foreign aid. On these items the young and the middle category are very similar in outlook.

While the relationships with respect to age and attitudes on economic welfare issues, race relations, and traditional foreign policy

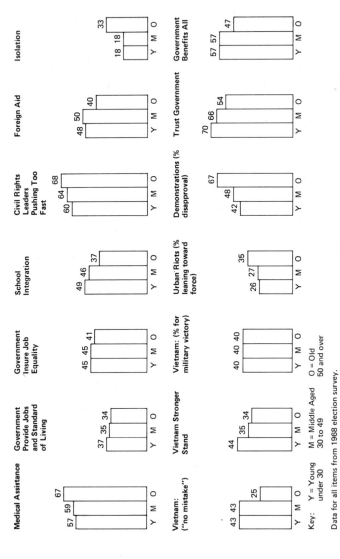

Key: Y = Young   M = Middle Aged   O = Old
      under 30   30 to 49   50 and over

Data for all items from 1968 election survey.

FIGURE 5.4. Age and opinions

items are not structured according to the generation gap hypothesis, the results are not too surprising. These are not particularly the types of issues over which one would expect youths to differ from their elders. Relationships between age and opinions in two other areas, however, offer more direct contradiction to popular expectations of how age might be expected to relate to political opinions. These issues are Vietnam and attitudes toward government. The popular picture of the past few years is one of youths very intensely opposed to the Vietnam involvement and increasingly cynical and disaffected from the government, and the older generation leaning toward the opposite positions on both types of issues. This picture has developed as a result of youths, especially college youths, having been the most visible protestors against the Vietnam war, having participated in the civil rights movement, having been the most likely to participate in radical groups of various types, and finally because of the role they played in the 1968 McCarthy movement and subsequent disruptions at the Democratic convention.

The data presented in Table 5.4 suggest a different situation. On the Vietnam question it is the oldest group that has demonstrated the greatest and most consistent opposition to the involvement. Those in the 50 and over category are most likely to say that the involvement was a mistake and least likely to support a stronger stand and military victory. Contrary to popular expectations, the young are consistently the most hawkish on this issue. These findings are fairly consistent with the findings of Gallup poll questions that have been posed about Vietnam over the past few years. The data from national surveys do not support the popular notion of the youths as disproportionately opposed to the war and older persons giving it massive support.

With respect to the governmental trust and the governmental benefit items, the findings again suggest that it is the older citizens who are most deviant from other groupings. They are also the most negative about the government. Of the oldest grouping, 54 percent said that the government could be trusted all or most of the time; 70 percent of those under 30 and 66 percent of those 30 to 49 took that position; 57 percent of both the young and middle group responded that the government works for the benefit of all of the people, whereas only 47 percent of those in the 50 and over category took that position.

On the urban riot item, those over 50 were somewhat more likely to support the use of force. The youths supported force in proportions very similar to those of the middle grouping. On the demonstration issue the pattern is much the same.

Although these findings do not suggest that age is significant in structuring political conflict over a wide range of issues, they strongly suggest that it is with respect to the oldest—not the youngest—that the opinion differences occur. There appears to be an underlying consistency of a relatively higher level of opposition to the Vietnam involvement, less support for civil rights efforts, strong disapproval of demonstrations, more negative reactions to the general proposition of U.S. international involvement, and greater unhappiness with the government. The older people go along with the farmers and the skilled workers as the groupings most disaffected from government and many national policies. Youths may have been the most vocal and visible in their discontent and opposition to certain policies, but dissatisfaction and disaffection seem more prevalent among those at the other end of the age or generation spectrum.

The discrepancy between these findings and the popular notions implied by the generation gap conception may result from several factors. First, though the age of 30 is generally given as the break-off point in reference to the generation gap, many of the attitudes, concerns, and spokesmen for the younger generation are probably concentrated in the prevoting age category (16 or 17 through 20) who were not represented in most national sample surveys prior to 1971. Second, many of the particular values, sentiments, and outlooks which are assumed to differentiate the youth from the older generation may be associated in fact with only one segment of the young—college youths. College youths make up only a minority of the youth; yet their activities, values, and articulations often are taken as the expression of youth in general. Third, differences between youths and adults along the lines suggested by the popular generation gap notions are probably most likely to appear with respect to issues and opinion areas other than those we have been considering here. To stress that there are not differences between youth and others on national political issues may be missing part of the point with respect to generation gap considerations. The differences between the generations may be more apparent with respect to social norms, behavioral patterns, and morality, rather than on questions of governmental welfare policies and international involvement.

A survey done for CBS News and used in a series of CBS television broadcasts on the generation gap in the summer of 1969 came up with data that speak to the points raised above.[5] The survey included four basic samples. First, there was a sample of college youths. Second, it included a national sample of youths between 17 and 23 who were not in college. Third, one-half of the parents of the college students were sampled. Fourth, an attempt was made to interview a sample of one-half of the noncollege youths. Three types of findings from this study are relevant to the points we are discussing here. First, on a great many issues, including some items on societal values, there were no great differences among the several samples. Second, with respect to many issues there were significant differences between the two youth samples, with the college youths tending to take the more liberal, radical, or permissive attitude, and the noncollege youths tending to fall in the opposite direction. For example, whereas only 35 percent of the college youths reported thinking that patriotism was "very important," 60 percent of the noncollege youths took that position.[6] Because the college and noncollege youths were weighted according to their proportions in the population, the percentage answering very important for the total youth sample was 55.

Third, on a number of issues there was a tendency for the noncollege youths to have opinion distributions very similar to those of the parental generation. That is, the gap was not so much between the young and the older generation as between the college youths and others, including the noncollege youths. This pattern was evident with respect to a question concerning the relative emphasis placed on equality versus law and order. The item was worded: "There is too much concern with equality and too little with law and order." The respondent could "strongly agree," "partially agree," or "strongly disagree." The percent "strongly agreeing" among the several samples was as follows:[7]

Total youth	College youth	Noncollege youth	Total parents	Parents college youth	Parents noncollege youth
42%	17%	48%	55%	42%	59%

The college youths are clearly the deviant group in responses to this item. The opinion distribution of the noncollege youths is much closer to that of the parents than it is to that of the fellow age cohorts who are in college. Note, also, the relatively small impact the college distribution has upon the distribution for the total youth sample.

THE STRUCTURING OF CONTEMPORARY
OPINION DISTRIBUTIONS

In this and the preceding chapter we have attempted to ascertain the extent to which distributions of political opinions are structured by several different social and geographic conditions. We have investigated the extent and patterns with which social-economic position, geographic region, race, and age structure opinion differences in a variety of policy issue areas.

The findings that are most significant for an understanding of the contemporary political disarray, as well as the future of American political life, have to do with the impact of social-economic position and of race. With respect to social-economic position, we have found that factors such as occupation and income seem to play only a minor role in the structuring of contemporary political divisions. Although there is some tendency for people in different occupations to have somewhat different opinion distributions with respect to economic welfare-industrial relations issues, the level of association between social-economic position and opinions in this area has decreased since the 1930s, 1940s, and early 1950s. With respect to the newer issues such as Vietnam, race relations, public order, and attitudes toward government, occupation and income show very little association with differences of opinion. On few issues in the contemporary period does occupation or income level seem to be very important in determining political opinions or preferences. As was indicated in the preceding chapter, the association seems to have remained the strongest with respect to what we have called conventional foreign policy concerns.

An important "destructuring" of political divisions and issue preferences according to social-economic divisions seems to have taken place over the last decade or so. The political coalitions and patterns of conflict, based largely on economic differences, which were welded together during the Depression and early days of the New Deal, seem to be coming apart. It has become less accurate to view issue and electoral struggles largely as conflicts between the "haves" and the "have-nots," the rich and the poor, the manual workers and the white-collar workers. These divisions which played an important part in structuring political life and our perceptions of politics over the past few decades appear less politically relevant today.

These changes have contributed to the contemporary disarray and confusion in American politics. Economic groups that have served as significant reference points for understanding and determining political preferences now often do not provide clear political guidelines. Groups such as organized labor, business, and manufacturing associations, and other groups that have been associated with the interests and values of particular economic groups, seem not to have consistent patterns of relationships with each other, with parties and political leaders, and with contemporary issues and policies. Labor unions and union leaders which often provided solid and consistent guidelines for their members as well as instruments for pressure on economic and welfare issues are divided on issues such as Vietnam and race. Labor leaders may praise the Republican president for taking a strong stand on law and order or campus unrest one day. The next day they may castigate him for mismanagement of the economy. Lower-middle-class suburbanites may praise the president one day because of his stand against forced bussing of schoolchildren for purposes of racial balance. They may condemn him the next day for not acting faster to stem the tide of inflation and unemployment. Some businessmen and professionals may feel very negative about the president because he did not withdraw American forces from Vietnam rapidly enough; other businessmen and professionals may be more inclined to praise him for holding on in Vietnam to defend American honor and for not surrendering to the enemy there or to the protesters at home. Political strategists may vary from day to day with regard to whether the Republican party should attempt to woo the skilled and industrial workers by stressing a hard line on crime, public order, and race, or concentrate on solidifying strength among their traditional source of support among business and professional people, or whether at the present time across-the-board appeals can be made effectively to any of the traditional social and economic groupings on any collection of issues or programs.

An explanation of the forces behind the waning impact of social-economic position in determining and structuring political opinions is beyond our purview at this point. The points we wish to stress here are that to a considerable extent economic positions seem relatively unimportant in structuring political differences at the present time and that the waning of the relevance of these factors in structuring and defining much of political life is one of the factors contributing to the existing disarray and confusion which we have discussed earlier. This "destructuring" probably has important long-range implications for the structure and substance of political parties and elections.

Race, on the contrary, was found to structure political opinions to a very considerable degree. The most extensive variations between blacks and whites in political outlooks are with items dealing with race relations and economic welfare type issues, but differences also are evident in most other policy areas. The questions of race relations and differences between blacks and whites in political interests and values seem to permeate nearly all aspects of contemporary political life. Aspects of the Vietnam involvement, welfare issues, crime and public order, governmental trust and responsiveness, urban development, and even issues surrounding the environmental issue have become inter-twined with the question of race and racism. As we pointed out earlier, however, the relatively small number of blacks means that they alone do not account for much of the structuring of political opinions within the overall population.

With respect to geographic region and age the analysis discussed above suggested that the basic geographic regions do not now play much of a role in structuring opinion on national policy issues and that age does not structure political differences to the extent and in the pattern which popular notions of the generation gap would predict. On most of the issues it is the older citizens, those over fifty, who deviate most from the other age groupings and who are most apt to feel negative about contemporary government and policies. Even on questions pertaining to race, the issue around which differences between the South and the rest of the nation have centered for more than a century, interregional differences in opinion distributions are small and seem to have decreased over the past two decades.

A similar lack of relationship is evident with respect to one additional factor which often has structured political identifications and outlooks in American society. This factor is religious and ethnic identification. During most of American history religious and ethnic affiliations have tended to be associated with partisan identifications and policy preferences. Persons from Irish, Italian, and Polish Catholic backgrounds, for example, have tended to identify with the Democratic party, often regardless of their own economic position. Jews, especially those who migrated from Eastern Europe at the end of the nineteenth and early twentieth centuries, also have exhibited a strong propensity to identify with the Democratic party. During the twentieth century, especially during and immediately following the depression of the 1930s, Catholics and Jews seemed to be more supportive of the New Deal and general government welfare measures. Alford, in his book *Party and Society*, argued that the political relevance of religious and ethnic identifications constituted one of the factors that worked to deflate the impact of class upon American political life.[8] Political perspectives tied to religious and ethnic identities have often cut across occupation and economic lines. We have not discussed, or extensively analyzed, the extent to which these affiliations help to structure political opinions today. A simple analysis, using 1968 and 1970 SRC data, relating opinion distributions to religion found that the opinion distriubtions among Catholics and Protestants were quite similar on almost all of the issue items. Nonidentifiers and Jews tended to be more liberal on most of the issues, but there were too few of each in these categories in the samples to allow for systematic and reliable comparisons. Although a comparison of Catholics and Protestants is only a crude measure of the role of religious and ethnic affiliation, the consistent pattern of no difference seems enough evidence to suggest that on the types of national policy issues we have been looking at, religious affiliation is not significant in shaping and structuring political preferences and differences. For example, on the medical assistance question, 59 percent of the Protestants and 60 percent of the Catholics in the 1968 survey reported favoring the proposition of government assistance. On the black job equality item, 43 percent of the Protestants and 41 percent of the Catholics favored action by the federal government. Thirty-nine percent of the Protestants and 36 percent of the Catholics favored getting tougher, as their responses to the item asking what should be done in Vietnam indicate.

Geography, religious-ethnic identities, and social-economic categories—the structures that have in the past tended to give structure and shape to our politics and to serve as important reference points for determining political preferences, values, and allegiances—seem to be losing their potency. Increased affluence, the spread of mass media, the nationalization of much of economic, political, and social life, and the change in issue concerns have tended to make these factors less relevant in contemporary political life. Among the several factors that we have looked at, race alone seems to structure differences in political outlooks to any considerable degree.

The waning influence of such conditions as social-economic position, regionalism, and religion in giving structure and meaning to political opinions and political conflicts is certainly a major contributor to the contemporary disarray and confusion. As Lane anticipated, many of the social and economic divisions that were important in an earlier period have lost their potency in determining political conflicts and providing a sense of urgency to political choices and outcomes. Contrary to Lane's prediction, however, there continue to be areas of considerable conflict. On issues of race relations, Vietnam, public order, and attitudes toward government, the public seems deeply and in some instances rather evenly divided. These conflicts and differences, however, do not follow the traditional patterns of structure. Consequently there is considerable confusion and flux and few stable coalitions or patterns of relationship apparent.

Notes

[1] V. O. Key, Jr., *Public Opinion and American Democracy* (New York: Knopf, 1961), p. 105.

[2] Op. cit., pp. 101–105.

[3] *Gallup Political Index* No. 59 (May 1970), p. 5.

[4] Gerhard Lenski, *Power and Privilege* (New York: McGraw-Hill, 1967).

[5] CBS News, *Generation Apart* (New York: Columbia Broadcasting System, 1969).

[6] Ibid., p. 10.

[7] Ibid., p. 26.

[8] Robert Alford, *Party and Society* (Chicago: Rand McNally, 1963), pp. 219–250.

CHAPTER 6
POLITICIZATION AND
POLITICAL OPINIONS

In the preceding two chapters we have investigated how political opinions are distributed according to a variety of social, economic, and geographic structures. In this and the following chapter we turn to the relationships between several political factors and the distributions of political opinions. In this chapter we inquire into the extent to which persons with different levels of political interest, involvement, and activity differ in political preferences. Or, phrasing the question in another way, to what extent are differences in political opinions structured by variations in the level of politicization? In the next chapter we inquire into the relationship between party identification and voting and opinion distributions.

Studies of voting and political behavior have discovered that there are wide variations in the extent to which people are active and involved in political life. Even in national presidential elections in the United States only about 60 percent of those potentially eligible actually vote. The turnout rates are considerably lower for off-year congressional and for state and local elections. When one considers other types of electoral behavior, such as campaigning for a candidate or attending political meetings, he finds himself dealing with only a small minority of the adult population. Only a small proportion of the public can be designated as active or very much involved in electoral politics.

Those who are active in politics are, by and large, more likely to have a greater impact on the political life and decisions of the nation than are those who are less active. The political process is more likely to respond to those who express their interests and voice their opinions through voting and other forms of political activity than to those who do not engage in these activities or express interest in politics. An interpretation of the operation of American politics based on these assumptions has been developed over the past few decades, as the extent and structure of political participation and involvement have become clearer.[1] Taking the empirical findings that participation and interest are not universally, nor even very widely engaged in by the citizenry, and that this condition puts disproportionate influence in the hands of the minority that does, this interpretation emphasizes that it is the interest, norms, and preferences of those who are active that largely determine how the system operates. Key argues that this small group of political activists, and how they interact with the rest of the public, is the key to understanding how American government operates within the context of public opinion.[2]

If political participation and interest are not widespread, and if those who are more active have greater influence in politics, the question of how the opinions and preferences of the more active compare with those who are less active becomes very important. The implications for the relationship between mass public opinion and government policy would be one thing if the preferences and values of the activists were quite dissimilar from those of the less active, and something quite different if the active and the less active tended to share political outlooks and interests. For example, if those who are active and most influential tend to be primarily conservative on domestic welfare issues, while the nonactivists tend to be primarily liberal on the same issues, one might expect to find that policies put into effect are more conservative than what might be preferred by the bulk of the public. It may be recalled that this is precisely the situation that Key found in the South in the mid-1950s. The votes of southern congressional represen- tatives and much of the rhetoric of southern political leaders tended to be conservative, more conservative than the popular preferences suggested by the distributions of opinion among the southern populace. Key explained this discrepancy, in part, by noting that political participation in the South has been particularly small and that the minority who participate tend to be disproportionately conservative on economic issues.[3] Southern political leaders and "representatives" simply reflect this set of biases.

These issues are important for understanding the operation and policy biases in American politics. They suggest that it is very important to know something about the opinions and preferences of the minority of activists as well as the preferences of the mass public, and about the similarities and differences in opinion distributions among different "political strata." In this chapter we attempt to see how political opinions are distributed according to several aspects of political participation and involvement. What are the patterns of relationship in the current period? Have there been changes in these relationships over the past few years? Finally, we look at the relationship between political activity, social-economic position, and political outlooks in order to ascertain whether relationships between activism and policy position are independent, or merely an artifact of the relationship between social-economic position and policy position. Conceptually and operationally the analytical task here is similar to that of the preceding two chapters. In the same way we sought to discover whether people in different occupations or income categories tend to have different opinion distributions, we wish to ascertain whether persons in different political strata tend to exhibit different opinion distributions. In the same way that one can talk about different economic strata, one can refer to different political strata.

The SRC election surveys have included items that permit the construction of indices of three dimensions of politicization or political stratification. These several dimensions are (1) electoral participation, (2) campaign involvement, and (3) political efficacy. These are the three indicators used by Key in his analysis of the impact of political stratification.[4] By using similar measures we can compare findings for the present period with those of a decade and a half earlier.

In each of its major election surveys the Survey Research Center has asked a number of questions in its postelection survey about what types of campaign or electoral activities the respondent participated in, as well as ascertaining whether or not the respondent voted. Using the 1968 survey, we constructed an index of electoral participation which divides the respondents into four participation categories or strata. At the low end of the scale are those who reported neither voting nor engaging in any of the other electoral-oriented activities. Next, there is a category that includes those who reported having voted but not having engaged in any of the other activities. There are two categories for those who reported having participated in campaign activities by doing things other than voting. In a moderately active category are those who reported that they talked to people and tried to persuade them how to vote, that they wore a campaign button, or did both of these things, but did not engage in any of the other activities that involved a higher level of commitment. The most active category includes those who reported having done one or more of the following: gave money or bought tickets to help in a campaign; attended a political meeting, rally, dinner, or the like; worked for one of the parties or candidates; or belonged to a political club or organization. The distinctions and rationale for these categories should be fairly clear. Going up the participation scale, each category is presumed to involve more effort, cost, and sense of commitment on the part of the respondent. The distributions of respondents in the 1968 study falling in the various categories are as follows:[5]

Category	%	(N)
1. Most active	17%	226
2. Moderately active	26%	349
3. Voted only	38%	506
4. Nonvoters, nonactivity	19%	250

The second dimension of politicization used here, political involvement, is basically a measure of concern with the presidential election. It is a combination of responses to two items. The first item asked the respondent whether he personally cared about the outcome of the election. The second item asked how much attention the respondent paid to the political campaign taking place that year. The responses to the two items are combined in such a way that the respondents who reported being personally very much concerned with the outcome of the election and paying very much attention to the election campaign were rated as the most involved. The individual not at all concerned with the outcome and who did not pay attention to the campaign ranked low. Other combinations of responses put the respondent somewhere in between. For analysis and presentation here the respondents were divided into five categories ranging from high involvement to low involvement. The response frequencies for the various categories of involvement are as follows:

The third dimension of politicization is political efficacy. This is a

Category	%	(N)
1. High involvement	13%	(196)
2. Moderately high	19%	(301)
3. Medium involvement	29%	(446)
4. Moderately low	26%	(401)
5. Low involvement	14%	(211)

concept and index developed by the Survey Research Center and used in all of its election studies. It attempts to measure the extent to which an individual feels he has an effect upon the political world. Do political leaders pay attention to him, or to people like him? Can people like him understand what goes on in politics? The index is constructed from responses to four items which pose questions similar to those just mentioned. It has been found to correlate very highly with various forms of political behavior as well as with interest and involvement in politics. The respondents were assigned ratings ranging from 1 to 5, based upon the number of the four items which they responded to in ways indicating an efficacious position. Thus, those who answered all four items in an efficacious manner rank 1 or highest. Those who answered all four items in ways indicating a lack of efficacy fall in category 5, lowest. The distribution of respondents falling in the various index positions for the years 1960 and 1968 are as follows:

Category	1960		1968	
	%	(N)	%	(N)
1. High	11%	(210)	15%	(194)
2.	31%	(592)	26%	(350)
3.	30%	(583)	18%	(246)
4.	18%	(339)	20%	(268)
5. Low	10%	(199)	21%	(284)

The 1960 responses are included here along with the 1968 frequencies to point out changes that have occurred in the level of political efficacy over the past decade. From 1960 to 1968 the proportion of respondents falling at the low end of the scale increased by 13 percentage points (categories 4 and 5 combined). There is not much change at the high end of the index. These data indicate a shift toward greater feelings of lack of political efficacy during the 1960s.

This pattern of change is congruent with other shifts in attitude toward government and its responsiveness that we discussed in Chapter 2. The decrease in feelings of political efficacy is an additional indicator of the growing disaffection from government and politics which we have noted at several points in our discussion.

These several measures of politicization are fairly highly correlated with each other. Persons with higher levels of political efficacy are likely to be more highly involved in elections and to participate more in the electoral process. Those who have a greater sense of involvement are more likely to participate, and vice versa. Key, using 1956 data, also found that each of these measures is highly correlated to an index of issue familiarity, an index that measured the extent to which persons were familiar enough with issues to have some sort of position on them.[6] These various interrelationships indicate that these several measures are tapping a common underlying factor that we refer to as politicization.

The concern of this chapter is the relationships between political strata and the distribution of issue opinions. A concern with the differential influence of persons with different opinions suggests that the relationship between opinions and level of electoral participation might be the most relevant set of relationships to look at. The bar graphs in Figure 6.1 give the relationships between level of electoral participation and opinions on fourteen issues using data from the 1968 SRC survey.

With respect to the economic welfare type issues the data in the figure indicate that the nonvoters are the most liberal on these issues, or most likely to support government action. Those in the most active category are the least likely to support the measures, but for both items the greatest variation is found between the nonvoters and the rest of the respondents. Especially with respect to the job and standard of living guarantee, there are almost no differences between the three categories representing voters and those who engaged in some form of electoral activity in addition to voting.

These findings are generally consistent with those of Key. Using a scale made up of several 1956 SRC items dealing with government economic and welfare activities, including medical assistance and job guarantee, Key reports that those with higher levels of participation are

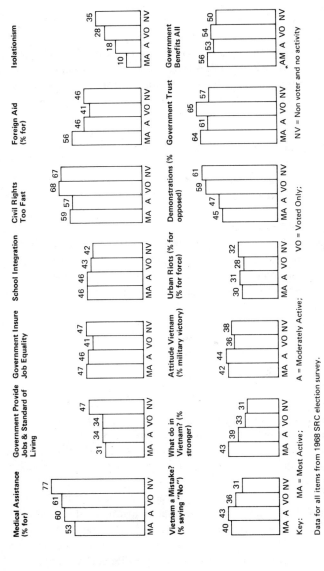

FIGURE 6.1. Electoral participation and issue opinions, 1968

Key: MA = Most Active;   A = Moderately Active;   VO = Voted Only;   NV = Non voter and no activity

Data for all items from 1968 SRC election survey.

somewhat more likely to oppose government activities. Those at the low participation end of the scale are slightly more likely to support them. Because the items measuring both opinions regarding welfare programs and electoral participation are not comparable, it is difficult to make accurate comparisons about the overall strength of relationships between 1956 and 1968. A rough comparison, however, seems to indicate that the range of difference in opinion between the activists, less active, and nonvoters on welfare state type issues is less in 1968 than in 1956. Although the relationships between political participation level and opinions on economic welfare issues are not strong, they do indicate a pattern that probably has some relevance for the types of opinions and interests that are most likely to be represented through the electoral process. Liberal preferences are most frequent among those who did not vote in 1968 and consequently are likely to have the least impact on the electoral process. Conversely, negative feelings about both medical assistance and job and standard of living guarantee were most frequent among those who were most active and likely to have the most impact on the electoral process. These patterns suggest a conservative bias to the electoral and policy-making processes.

It is difficult to draw very precise relationships between public policy and public opinion. A scattering of survey data on opinions during the 1940s and 1950s, however, does suggest that on a number of economic welfare type issues the general population was prepared to support programs of federal activity that political leaders and representatives did not put into policy until the mid-1960s. Public opinion poll data, for example, suggest that throughout most of the post–World War II period, a substantial majority of the public has endorsed the notion of and various specific programs involving federal aid to education and some form of government health assistance. The legislative enactments in both of these policy areas did not occur until 1965 when, after the Democratic landslide, a program of federal aid to education and the Medicare program for the aged were made into law. The legislative enactments of Congress are, of course, influenced by a wide range of conditions, including internal institutional arrangements. It seems reasonable to assume, however, that the tendency of the most active to be less likely than the less active to support new economic welfare measures would help account for the discrepancy between public support and legislative action.

Level of electoral participation makes little difference for opinions on the race relations issues. Persons in each of the four participation categories supported the school integration and black job propositions in very similar proportions. The less active respondents, however, were a little more likely than those who did more than vote to think that civil rights groups were pushing too fast. It is interesting to note that the same lack of relationship between differences in political participation and opinions on the school intergration and black job questions is evident, with only slight variations, within each of the major geographic regions. The largest variation occurs in the Northeast where the most active are the most supportive and the nonvoters the least supportive of the two propositions.

This pattern of responses with respect to the race issue is consistent with that noted in earlier chapters. On the race issue the population is substantially and fairly evenly divided. At least with respect to the school integration question, the same close division has continued since the mid-1950s. The question of race and especially actions of the federal government to attempt to bring about racial integration and equality are among the most salient and emotionally intense issues in the current period. The opinion divisions on these issues, however, are not structured to any considerable extent by any of the several factors that have tended to shape political divisions in the immediate past. The important exception is, of course, race itself. Occupation, income, age, religious identification, and level of electoral participation are at the most only very slightly related to differences of opinion on these racial questions. Even variations in opinion between southerners and others are not very great.

Those in the most active category are the most likely to endorse traditional foreign affairs involvement items. Fifty-six percent of those in the most active category supported the foreign aid proposition. Support for the program among the other three participation groupings is very similar, 10 to 15 percentage points below that of the most active category. On the more abstract isolationism issue there is a patterned and fairly significant relationship. The higher the level of electoral participation the more likely one is to reject the isolationist proposition. The pattern of relationship is ordered and progressive. While only 10 percent of those in the most active category endorsed the isolationist proposition, 18 percent of the moderately active, 28 percent of those who voted only, and 35 percent of the nonvoters took that position. These findings also are similar to those of Key's earlier analysis. Using a foreign issue scale, composed of several items from the 1956 SRC survey, Key found that the high participants were somewhat more likely to take an internationalist position than were those who participated less.[7] Support for international involvement comes disproportionately from those who are more active and involved. Those less active are more apt to be opposed or apathetic toward international involvement and international concerns in general. It is interesting to note that for electoral participation as with occupation, income, and age the strongest association with issue opinions is in the area of these traditional foreign policy items.

There is a small relationship between level of electoral participation and attitudes toward the Vietnam involvement. The same patterns exist with respect to all three items. Those who reported having done more than vote were more likely to say that we did not make a mistake getting involved in Vietnam and more likely to support escalation or the notion of a military victory than were those who reported that they voted only or that they did not even vote. Unlike the pattern with respect to welfare state type issues and the traditional foreign affairs issues the important dividing point on the Vietnam items was between the two active categories and the two least active categories. The differences between the several participation levels are not large, but the essential pattern is there. Attitudes favoring the involvement in Vietnam, like other forms of international involvement, were most highly concentrated among the most active and seemingly most influential segments of the public.

The patterning of opinions on the two public order type issues was different. On the urban riot issue there were no differences among the participation groupings. Within each of the categories slightly less than a third leaned toward the use of force. The lack of differentiation here is similar to that noted with respect to the race relations issues. This similarity probably results in part from the tendency of many people to view the urban riots as a component of the racial question.

With respect to the demonstration issue there is a somewhat different pattern. Those in the two most active categories are somewhat less likely to disapprove of the use of demonstrations than are the less active. There is a 16 percentage point range between the frequency of opposition among the most active and that among the least active group. The variation in response patterns between the urban riot and demonstration items probably stems from the fact that on the urban riot issue racial attitudes come into play, while on the demonstration issue questions of civil liberties and the toleration of dissent become involved.

A number of studies have documented the important tendency for those who are more active in politics—for example, the political activists, the political influentials, and political leaders—to be more supportive of civil liberty positions and of basic democratic norms than are the less active citizens. Key found this pattern in his public opinion analysis, using an item asking whether persons accused of being Communists should be fired from government positions.[8] Herbert McClosky has investigated these relationships more extensively.[9] Using a sample of influentials (delegates to the 1956 Democratic and Republican conventions) and a sample of the general electorate, he compared responses to a wide range of issues concerning support for basic liberties and democratic principles. He found support for these norms or principles consistently higher among the influentials than among the general public. Unfortunately the SRC surveys and other data sources we are using here do not include other items containing civil liberty type components. We would suspect, however, that the same general pattern holds for such issues today. That is, those who are more politically active would tend to be more supportive of civil liberty positions and more sympathetic toward the rights of dissenters to express their opinions.

On the two items measuring attitudes toward government, there is surprisingly little correlation between level of political participation and opinion distributions. On the governmental trust question there is a slight tendency for the least active to be a bit less trusting. On the governmental benefit item there is only a slight tendency for the most active to be more likely to say that government works for the benefit of all, and for those in the nonvoter category to be least likely to take that position. These relationships, again, are very slight, not large enough to suggest any significant ordering.

One might have anticipated that those who participated more in the electoral and campaign process would be more likely to regard the system with trust, and those who did not participate much, to see the system operating more to serve the interests of the few. Such has probably been the relationship in the past. We suspect that for a number of reasons one of the changes that has taken place in the present period of frustration, disaffection, and disarray is an increase in the amount of dissatisfaction and growing lack of political trust on the part of many of those who have been more active in politics. This change would include many of the "doves" who have been unhappy about the Vietnam involvement and frustrated because they were not able to alter that policy; the politically involved local union leader who is unhappy over what he perceives as the government's increased attention to the blacks, often at his expense; the small-town business-man-civic leader who is frightened by the growing power of the federal government and the increased attention placed upon urban problems; and the liberal professional who feels disillusioned by the lack of "real" change in the conditions of the poor and minority groups despite the liberal programs and promises. These are all types of people who generally have been active in politics, but who over the past few years have found reasons to become disenchanted with the operation of government and the results of political action.

Let us review briefly the patterns discerned thus far. The least active were *somewhat* more likely to support the liberal propositions on economic welfare type issues and least internationalist on the traditional foreign policy issues. The more active respondents were a *little* more likely than the less active to sanction the involvement in Vietnam and to support hard line positions. With respect to the race relations items, the urban riot question, and attitudes toward govern-mental trust and responsiveness, there were no relationships between level of electoral participation and opinion. Although we have only a little evidence from the data we are using to support the proposition, it seems that the more active are more likely to support civil liberty positions and to be tolerant of dissent. The relationships are not very strong. In no instance can it be said that the level of participation is a major factor in structuring issue conflict. In no instance is there a situation in which the opinions of the participants are skewed strongly to one side and the nonparticipants to the other side. However, inasmuch as electoral participation serves as one of the means by which the opinions and interests of the citizenry can have an impact on the actions of government, even relatively small differences can be significant in determining the relationship between public opinion and public policy. For example, opponents of extending government economic welfare and industrial relations programs, particularly in the past, may have been able to compensate for their relative weakness in numbers with their greater tendency to vote and to participate in activities that have greater influence on what government does. The condition of strong support among the vocal activists for foreign involvement and foreign economic aid may serve to counterbalance the opposition or apathy toward such action on the part of those less active in politics.

The same general patterns between opinion distributions and politicization are evident with respect to the two other dimensions of politicization, political involvement and political efficacy, with some differences. The relationships between the involvement measure and the participation measure yield particularly similar results. These two measures both tap predispositions and activities concerning the presidential campaign and other elections. They are more highly related to each other than either of them is to the measure of political efficacy. With respect to the efficacy measure there are some different patterns. A few of these will be noted here. For the most part the correlations between efficacy and opinion tended to be somewhat stronger than those between participation or involvement and the opinion distributions. There was a tendency for level of political efficacy to order opinions on race relations and attitudes toward government. On the race issues the magnitude of association is still small. The direction is for the more efficacious person to be more likely to support civil rights and integration. Efficacy orders attitudes toward governmental benefits and trustworthiness more strongly. For example, while only 24 percent of those in the most efficacious category thought the government worked for the benefit of a few big interests, 57 percent of those in the lowest efficacy category took that position. This relationship should not be surprising. The governmental trust and government benefit items are getting at outlooks fairly similar to the type of citizen-government relationship tapped by the efficacy index itself.

For the foreign affairs issues the pattern is the same as with electoral participation, though the magnitude of the association is stronger. On the Vietnam issues those with higher efficacy differ from the others most by their tendency to choose middle-ground positions. Those ranking low on the scale are disproportionately likely to claim that the involvement in Vietnam was a mistake and to say that we should pull out or withdraw immediately.

With only a few exceptions, notably relationships pertaining to the attitudes toward government, efficacy seems to correlate to the several 1968 issues in patterns similar to the correspondence between social-economic position and the issues. Also, as was the case with income and occupation, the level of association between efficacy and opinions has decreased with respect to the economic welfare issues over the past decade and a half. The data presented in Table 6.1 show the level of association between political efficacy and opinions on six issues for 1956, 1960, 1964, and 1968. The gamma coefficients indicate that the extent to which variations in efficacy relate to opinion differences on the medical assistance and job guarantee issues decreases over the twelve-year period, though the relationship does not completely disappear. With respect to the school integration item there is a consistent nonrelationship for each of the three years. For the black job equality item there is a small relationship in 1956 which dissipated by 1960 and became nonexistent in 1968. With respect to the foreign aid

TABLE 6.1 Trends in relationship between political efficacy and selected political opinions, 1956–1968

	1956[a]	1960	1964	1968
Medical Assistance	.32	.31	.28	.21
Government Job Guarantee[b]	.30	.28	.20	.09
Black Job Equality	.11	.09	.00	.08
School Integration	.05	.05	.17	.09
Civil Rights Too Fast			.06	.09
Foreign Aid	.11	.11	.21	.29
Isolationism	.36	.38		.54
Was Vietnam a Mistake?			.32	.22
What Do Now in Vietnam?			.12	.12
Trust Government			.26	.28
Government Benefit			.28	.24

Source: Data from the 1956, 1960, 1964, and 1968 SRC surveys.

[a] The measure of association reported here is the gamma coefficient. See Appendix B for a brief discussion of this measure. The same trends over time are ascertained when Kendall's tau and Pearson correlations are computed.

[b] The questions in the 1964 and 1968 surveys are worded considerably differently and elicited different patterns of responses. So the coefficients for 1964 and 1968 cannot be considered strictly comparable with those of 1956 and 1960.

question the opposite trend is apparent. There is a steady increase in the level of association. The coefficients for the isolationism relationships indicate a consistently strong relationship throughout the several studies. At each of the three time points it is the item on which opinions are most highly structured by political efficacy. The reader may find it interesting to compare these findings with the very similar findings with respect to income and opinions presented in Table 4.6.

The similarities in the patterns of relationships between policy opinions and political stratification, on the one hand, and between these opinions and social-economic position, on the other hand, lead to the next question we wish to raise. This is the interrelationships between opinions, political stratification, and social-economic position. To what extent are social-economic position and level of political participation, involvement, and efficacy related? If they are related, to what extent are the relationships found between politicization and opinion distributions caused simply by the relationships between social-economic position and opinions?

In Table 6.2, data are presented showing the relationship between political participation and occupation of head of household. There is a moderately strong tendency for the level of participation to be ordered by the occupation categories. The professionals are the most active, with 55 percent reporting having done more than vote in 1968. Thirty-eight percent of the skilled workers and 39 percent of the nonskilled workers fell in the two more active categories. Although

TABLE 6.2 The relationship between occupation of head and level of electoral participation, 1968

	Level of Electoral Participation			
Occupation	HIGH	MODERATELY HIGH	VOTE ONLY	NONVOTER
Professional-Technical	28%	27%	35%	10%
Business-Managers	20	33	35	12
Clerical and Sales	21	23	44	12
Skilled Workers	12	26	40	22
Nonskilled Workers	13	26	36	24
Farmers	23	23	46	9

Source: Data used in these computations are from the 1968 SRC election survey.

there is a pattern of gradual decrease in level of participation as one moves from category to category down the occupation ladder, the most substantial difference occurs between the nonmanual occupations (professionals, businessmen, managers, clerical and sales workers) and the manual occupations. There are almost no differences between the two manual worker categories. The farmers and the clerical-sales workers fall in between the manual workers and the professional and business people but are closer to those at the top of the occupational hierarchy than to those at the bottom. Occupation orders the level of electoral participation in a stronger and more consistent way than it does almost any of the policy questions.

Social-economic position also tends to order the two other indices of politicization. The magnitude of the relationships is considerably stronger for the political efficacy index than for the involvement index. These relationships seem to have remained consistently high over the past decade and a half. Table 6.3 shows the gamma coefficients computed between income and education and political efficacy and political involvement for survey data from 1956, 1960, 1964, and 1968. Note the high association between both education and income and political efficacy. Although there are some fluctuations from year to year the data do not suggest any consistent movement toward a weakening of the association. Higher levels of efficacy are rather strongly associated with higher educational attainment and higher income. The same pattern is evident in the association between political involvement and education and income. The strength of association, however, is not as strong.

Differences in level of politicization are related to issues in a variety of

TABLE 6.3 Income/education vs. political efficacy and political involvement: 1956, 1960, 1964, and 1968

	1956[a]	1960	1964	1968
Political Efficacy				
Family Income	.34	.27	.31	.28
Education Level	.48	.38	.42	.42
Political Involvement				
Family Income	.16	.17	.14	.16
Education Level	.19	.24	.24	.23

Source: Data from SRC surveys, 1956, 1960, 1964, 1968.
[a] The measure of association reported here is the gamma coefficient. See Appendix B for a brief discussion of this measure. The same trends over time are ascertained when Kenndall's tau and Pearson correlations are computed.

patterns. These patterns of relationship are quite similar to those found between social-economic position and opinions on the same policies. Changes over the past decade or so in the extent and patterning of these relationships are also very similar. There is a decrease in the level of association with respect to both of these measures and traditional economic welfare types issues and no significant changes in the lack of association between social-economic position or politicization and the school integration item. Both higher social-economic status and higher participation and involvement are positively associated with support for international involvement throughout the period from the mid-1950s through the 1960s. Relationships with the foreign aid question increase over the same time period.

The fact that the patterns of relationship are so similar and that they change in the same way over time suggests that the impact of social-economic position and politicization may not be independent of each other. It is quite possible that the relationships found between political stratification and opinions result not so much from any independent influence that political participation and involvement have, but rather from the fact that those who are more active and involved tend to come disproportionately from the higher income and occupation groupings. Businessmen and professionals are somewhat less likely than manual workers to support propositions such as government medical assistance. They are also more likely to participate in electoral and political activities. It could be that the political activity and involvement do not affect the preferences of businessmen with respect to proposals such as the medical assistance proposition, but rather that the professional or businessman develops his opposition to such programs on the basis of his economic interests and position and simply carries it with him as he engages in political actions. Similarly, manual workers tend to be more concentrated in the lower categories of political action and involvement. They also have been more likely to support government economic welfare and regulation policies. The tendency for those exhibiting lower levels of political participation and involvement to be more supportive of welfare type measures may simply reflect this concentration of manual workers with their more liberal outlooks. The extent of participation or involvement may in this sense have little independent impact.

Let us restate these issues in the form of questions that can be investigated with the data we have available. The key question is whether the relative conservatism of the most active in regard to economic welfare issues, their greater tendency to support international involvement, their greater likelihood to endorse the involvement in Vietnam as well as support stronger action there, the tendency not to oppose demonstrations and the like result from greater participation, or are merely artifacts of the strong relationship between occupation and electoral participation. Do highly active manual workers tend to share the outlooks of other high participants, or are they closer in outlook to their fellow manual workers? Do nonvoting professionals and businessmen share the more liberal outlooks of their fellow nonvoters, or are their outlooks more strongly influenced by their feelings of economic interest and solidarity with their fellow professionals or businessmen?

We can begin to sort out these relationships and to formulate answers to these questions by taking the various occupation groupings and seeing how much variation there is on issues among the participation levels within each occupation. We have done this with the major policy issues from the 1968 SRC survey. Rather than present and discuss all of the data involved in this exercise we will summarize and interpret what seems to be the major thrust of the findings. Although the patterns are not altogether clear and consistent, it seems that, for the most part, it is occupation that makes the difference in determining the patterns of relationship between participation and issue preferences. The extent of relationship between participation and opinions within each of the occupation groupings is generally comparatively small and forms few consistent patterns. Nonskilled workers are more likely than others to support the government medical assistance proposition regardless of their level of electoral participation. White-collar workers are less likely to support the job guarantee proposition whether they have been relatively active or inactive in electoral politics.

Having stated the major proposition, let us qualify it by suggesting that there are some variations among the occupation groupings and issues that are both interesting and potentially significant. On the international involvement issues and the demonstration question, the level of participation appears to have an impact independent from that of occupation. Within the occupation groupings those who are more active are more apt to approve of demonstrations and to reject the isolationist proposition.

Participation level tended to order the opinions of the skilled workers more than for any other occupation. This was evident with respect to the welfare issues, attitudes toward government, and the isolation item. The more active skilled workers tended to be more conservative on the welfare issues, more positive toward government, and more supportive of international involvement than were non-participating skilled workers. Among the businessmen and professionals there were also some patterns, though the relationships were not as strong or consistent as those with the skilled workers. Among the professionals those in the most active category tended to be more liberal on the welfare issues, more supportive of civil rights and integration efforts, more likely to approve of demonstrations, and more supportive of international involvement than their less active professional cohorts. For businessmen the opposite was the case, particularly in regard to the economic welfare issues. Those businessmen who fell in the most active category were the most likely to take the conservative position. There were not consistent patterns among the clerical and sales people nor among the nonskilled manual workers.

Notes

[1] See, for example, Bernard Berelson, Paul Lazarsfeld, and William N. McPhee, *Voting* (Chicago: University of Chicago Press, 1964); Robert A. Dahl, *Who Governs?* (New Haven: Yale University Press, 1961); and V. O. Key, Jr., *Public Opinion and American Democracy* (New York, Knopf, 1963), chapter 21. For a critique of these interpretations see Peter Bachrach, *Theory of Democratic Elitism* (Boston: Little, Brown, 1967).

[2] Key, loc. cit.

[3] Ibid., pp. 101–105.

[4] Ibid., chapter 8.

[5] With respect to these and other turnout and participation data gathered through survey research the reader should keep in mind that surveys tend to come up with higher turnout percentages than voting returns and other estimates of voting. That is, a higher percentage of persons responding to postelection surveys report having voted than the percentages indicated by numbers of actual voters and population estimates.

[6] Ibid., p. 185.

[7] Ibid., p. 187

[8] Ibid., p. 188.

[9] Herbert McClosky, "Ideology and Consensus in American Politics," *American Political Science Review,* Vol. LVIII (June 1964), pp. 361–382.

CHAPTER 7
POLITICAL PARTIES, ELECTIONS, AND OPINIONS: THE PROBLEM OF POLITICAL RESPONSE AND POLITICAL CHANGE

Political life in the United States, as we have suggested before, is in a state of disarray and confusion. Changes are taking place and tensions forming within many associations, groupings, and coalitions which have given structure and meaning to American political life over the past few decades. The nation is confronted with new types of social, political, and economic issues. Some of these new issues generate considerable passion and conflict. These new conflicts tend to cut through the social structure in ways different from the conflicts of the immediate past. Social-economic groupings, ethnic and racial associations, political parties, and other political associations are being pulled asunder by new patterns of division and conflict. Many people are seeking important changes in political goals and processes. The growth in demand for political change has been followed, in many instances, by intense opposition to change and passionate support for traditional practices. These conflicts and hostilities have found expression in various slogans displayed on stickers placed on windows and car bumpers: "America, Love It or Leave It," "Peace Is Patriotic," "If Guns Are Outlawed, Only Outlaws Will Have Guns."

One important component of the contemporary discontent is the disillusion and frustration which many feel with regard to political institutions, processes, and leadership. In Chapter 2 we noted the substantial increases between 1964 and 1970 in the proportion of responses indicating a lack of trust in government and a belief that the government does not work for the benefit of all of the people. This sense of frustration stems, in part, from the seeming inability of government, political parties, political leaders, and electoral contests to come to grips with the demands for change and nonchange, to give them expression and meaning, and to respond to them in any coherent and decisive manner. To many who feel deeply about issues such as Vietnam, race relations, social justice, law and order, threats to political freedoms, or the changing of national priorities, the system has seemed unwilling or unable to respond. College youths and others who pressured for withdrawal from the Southeast Asia involvement, and sought to make that involvement the central political issue of the day, are only the most widely publicized example of those who feel frustrated by the seeming lack of response. Parents, in both the North and the South, who have protested against court-ordered bussing to bring about racial integration or racial balance in the public schools represent another segment of agitated and frustrated citizens. As we have pointed out previously, the skilled workers, older citizens, and farmers—all show relatively higher levels of distrust and frustration concerning government politics and responsiveness in comparison with other major population groupings.

The failure of effective response, or the sluggishness with which the political apparatus has reacted to current political demands and interests is what we refer to here as the problem of political response. There are deep and widespread disagreements over the course of social and political policy. Political leaders, the electoral system, and political parties seem to have unusual difficulty in relating to these new areas of conflict. The past few national elections seem to have resolved little with respect to what direction the nation is headed or in what direction the citizenry would like to move with respect to issues such as race relations, Vietnam, public order, proper national priorities. Legislative debates and skirmishes have resolved little and have failed to set any particular course of action clearly. The fact that both George McGovern and George Wallace proved popular vote getters in the 1972 Democratic primaries indicated that many people were unhappy with contemporary politics, but it did little to clarify in what direction the voters wanted the nation to move. It is our thesis that the sense of frustration and the difficulty in generating effective political response stem, in some measure, from the ways in which political parties and electoral coalitions interact with the various patterns of opinion distributions and issue conflicts which have come to the fore in the past decade. It is these relationships that we explore in this chapter. In the previous three chapters we have stressed how several of the social, economic, and demographic conditions that have often structured divisions in political opinions do not seem very relevant in structuring contemporary political interests and preferences. Here we wish to investigate the extent to which political parties and voting preferences are related to differences in political opinions.

In most "modern" societies the institutions that play the most important part in linking the interests, demands, and preferences of the mass citizenry with the governmental policy-making apparatus are political parties and elections. It is primarily through the electoral processes that the government is presumed to get its most significant pressures and directives from the population at large. Theorists of democracy and students of electoral politics may differ on how direct an impact the citizenry has on the actions of government, and, even on how much influence it should have. There is agreement, however, that it is through the electoral process that such an impact is to be felt. Nearly all forms of democratic theory hold that it is through the electoral system that the will of the people is to be expressed, the course of the polity determined or at least influenced, political leadership selected, and control exerted over the government by the governed. Whether the impact of elections on policy formation is direct or indirect, and even if elections serve only symbolic purposes, electoral contests are central to the relationships between people and government.

Closely related to elections in linking political opinions to government are political parties. In most democratic polities political parties have come to play important roles in the formation of political opinions and interests, in the structuring and expression of political conflict, and in the transmission of political demands and concerns into public policy. The recent literature and analysis of elections and opinion formation in the United States have stressed the important role of party and party identification in the formation of political preferences and values. Political party identification and party leaders serve as important reference points through which individuals develop and organize their own political outlooks. Stands taken by party leaders play a role in the formation of the political preferences of party identifiers.

Political parties have also been important in the articulation and structuring of political conflict. To some extent the question of which issues get discussed and become relevant in electoral contests is determined by the parties and party leadership. Issues of conflict or potential conflict may be either clearly articulated or hidden in electoral contests, according to how opinions on those issues are distributed among party leaders and supporters. Party leaders are likely to stress those issues that tend to unify their followers and to gain them new support. They will tend to avoid the clear articulation of issues that might divide their identifiers or potential supporters. Thus, through most of the first half of the twentieth century, the race issue was not articulated as part of national party or electoral contests.[1] Such an issue would tend to split the Democratic party, and it was not of much relevance to the Republican party. In the late 1950s and 1960s race became an important part of national electoral and party politics. Both parties, at least for a short time span, saw the potential of winning more votes than they were likely to lose by stressing and supporting civil rights efforts. The development of concern for racial justice among many people, the significant numbers of black voters in strategic locations in northern swing states where black voters might well determine election outcomes, and the support, or at least neutrality, of other segments of people in both parties made it possible and in many instances desirable for the parties to focus attention on programs designed to assure racial equality and integration. By the late 1960s and early 1970s this situation no longer existed. Support for increased activity in the civil rights field has diminished in the Republican party. The basic supporters of the Democratic party are very much divided over racial issues. It is likely that in the 1970s the parties, especially the Democratic party, will find it more advantageous to play down racial issues because attention on them will prove divisive to its basic support.

Political parties serve also as a means for transmitting the demands and concerns of various groups into the decision-making arenas. Different economic, ethnic, regional, and social groupings have looked variously toward one or the other parties to express and press for their interests. Since the 1930s labor organizations have, more often than not, relied on the Democratic party to express and support their interests. Business and commercial people have looked toward the Republican party. Until recently the South has looked toward the Democratic party to look after its interests. Farmers have tended to move back and forth between the parties as a means of pushing their particular economic interests. In the late 1950s and early 1960s the blacks tended to play off the parties in pressing civil rights concerns. Since 1964 they have been tightly wedded to the Democratic party.

We do not wish to imply that elections and political parties successfully or faithfully provided any or all of these functions all the time. The extent to which they serve as molders of opinions, structurers of political conflict, and transmitters of the interests and concerns of segments of the electorate varies from time to time. For a number of reasons it is particularly difficult for American elections and parties to serve as a direct and faithful mandate of popular opinion on many issues.[2] The point is that to the extent that the linkages between the mass public and the government get made, parties and elections play an important role.

At present we are in a situation in which parties and elections find it particularly difficult to give expression and structure to political conflicts and to represent and transmit in meaningful ways the interests and concerns of large parts of the populace. To reiterate, there are areas of considerable disagreement, demands for new policies, pressures for changes in focus and priorities, but there is little indication of meaningful political response. There has been instead increased discontent and frustration regarding both political parties and elections. We have already cited some indicators of the current nonresponse and the disaffection regarding parties and electoral outcomes. The outcome of congressional elections in 1968 constitutes another particularly telling example of the disparity between political concerns and electoral and party response.

The discontent and frustrations connected with the presidential election in 1968 are well known. The withdrawal of President Johnson from the race, the McCarthy movement, the assassination of Robert Kennedy, the troubles surrounding the Democratic convention in Chicago, the Wallace third party movement, and the nondecisiveness of the election outcome serve as vivid reminders of the passions and confusions that accompanied the presidential election that year. The outcome of contests for the House of Representatives, on the other hand, has received less attention. In contests for the 435 seats in the House only a total of 14 seats changed party hands in 1968. That is, only 3 percent of the seats switched from the control of one party to the other. The Republicans, at the same time they won control of the presidency, made a net gain of only four seats. This seems a remarkably high level of nonchange.

In the future, the casual observer of these results is likely to take such stability as indicating a high level of satisfaction with government and its policies. The figures may suggest to the future observer that most people were not interested in change in leadership or in alterations in policy, that 1968 was a time of consensus and high satisfaction. As we have stressed before, 1968 was not a period of contentment, especially with respect to political policies, political parties, and political leadership. Rather than reflecting widespread satisfaction with the status quo, the 1968 congressional election results reflect a significant lack of political (partisan, electoral, and leadership) response to the issues, concerns, fears, passions, and conflicts that were prevalent at the time. There was widespread concern among the citizenry about Vietnam, race relations, public order, crime in the streets, and government trust and credibility. The parties and electoral contests seem not to have reflected these concerns. It may not be too farfetched to suggest that, in many instances, contests for the House were somewhat irrelevant to the concerns and issues that were bothering large segments of the public. The congressional elections in 1970 and in 1972 offered little more in the way of a coherent, policy-relevant response. They gave little indication as to whether the citizenry preferred to move in a liberal or conservative direction, preferred the Republican or Democratic party, were content or discontent with the government in office, or how most people felt about the issues of race, Vietnam, or public order.

The extent to which elections and the positions articulated by political parties relate closely to the basic issue concerns and divisions among the citizenry depends, in some measure, on how political preferences and opinions on salient issues are distributed among the party identifiers and among the various groups that make up party supporters. The types of people that make up the support of a party and the distributions of opinions among those supporters make it easier for parties to structure, discuss, and respond to some types of issues more than others. For example, during the 1840s the American party system, which at that time centered around the Whig and Democratic parties, was more or less able to channel conflict and generate debate over issues such as the national bank, internal improvements, and the nature of the presidency. On these issues each party could rally and hold together important segments of its own supporters and mount opposition against the other party. The slavery issue, however, presented a very different situation. Both the leadership and the identifiers of the two parties were split, primarily along sectional (North-South) lines, on that issue. For some years both the Whigs and the Democrats had sought to submerge the smouldering issue of slavery and its extension into the new territories. They were able to do this with some success until the early 1850s. During the decade of the 1850s, however, people in both the North and the South became more and more agitated and divided over the slavery questions. The parties found it more and more difficult either to contain or respond to the issue. The results were the emergence of new party coalitions—first, the Free Soilers and, then, the Republican party, both of which took more direct and outspoken stands on the slavery question. Eventually these sectional divisions led to the splitting of both parties along sectional lines, and finally to the disappearance of the Whig party. In the 1860 election four parties ran candidates for president, and the new Republican party won the presidency. The eventual outcome of the sectional conflict, was of course, the Civil War.

This example represents an extreme situation, but it illustrates well the point we wish to make here. Whig-Democratic competition was structured around one set of issues and rested on a particular social base, one that cut across sectional lines. When new issues that divided the population along sectional lines became salient, the established parties with their particular appeals and coalitions became less relevant. The internal divisions kept them from responding effectively to the new salient issues. Eventually they were unable to organize the elections and contain or control policy divisions. Following the Civil War, a new party system developed with the Republican and Democratic parties as the key competitors. The geographic base and issue differences of the new party system were not the same as those that existed before the Civil War.

We have pointed out that the past decade has witnessed the development of new social and political issues, and these new issues relate to the social, economic, demographic, and geographic divisions in the population differently from the welfare and economic issues that were top priority during the previous decades. The question to be investigated now is how issue opinions in the contemporary period relate to differences in party identifications and electoral support. To what extent do party identifications tend to structure differences on issue positions? Do Republicans tend to line up on policy issues differently from Democrats? What about Independents? What about differences between opinion areas? Do Democrats and Republicans tend to divide on some issues and not on others?

Table 7.1 shows the comparisons between Democrats, Republicans, and Independents in their positions on sixteen issues from the 1968 SRC survey. In the preparation of these data, those falling in the Democratic category represent both the strong and the not-so-strong Democratic identifiers, according to the SRC seven-category party identification index.[3] The Republican category similarly includes both strong and weak Republican identifiers. The Independent category includes all of those who responded Independent when they were asked about party identification. Those who on further probing responded that they were closer to the Democratic or Republican party are included with the Independents. The figures in the column at the far right indicate the range of difference between the Democratic and Republican identifiers. The higher the range score the greater the interparty difference. The lower the score the closer or more similar the distributions.

The data indicate where clear differences between the party identifiers exist and where the opinion distributions are similar. It is evident from the data that differences in policy opinions between the supporters of the two parties are greatest on the traditional economic welfare type issues. Those who call themselves Democrats are more likely to support the medical assistance proposition, to support the government job and living guarantee idea, and to hold that the federal government is not getting too powerful. There are moderately strong

TABLE 7.1 Party identification and opinions on issues, 1968

Issue	Democrats	Independents	Republicans	Difference between Democrats and Republicans
Government Medical Assistance				
% in favor	76%	55%	41%	35
Government Job and Living Guarantee				
% in favor	46	27	25	21
Government Too Powerful				
% saying "Yes"	42	60	72	30
Government Promote Black Job Equality				
% for	52	38	35	17
Government Promote School Integration				
% for	51	38	35	16
Civil Rights Pushing Too Fast				
% agreeing	58	72	69	11
Foreign Aid				
% for	48	42	45	3
Isolationism				
% saying stay home	25	19	25	0
Vietnam Involvement a Mistake				
% saying a mistake	62	59	66	4
What Do Now in Vietnam?				
% for escalation	33	42	35	2
Attitude on Vietnam				
% leaning military victory	38	41	40	3

Urban Riots				
% leaning toward use of force	25	34	31	6
Demonstrations				
% expressing disapproval	53	52	56	3
Government Listen to People				
% great deal of time	26	22	23	3
Trust Government to Do Right				
% trusting all or most of the time	67	57	62	5
Government Benefits				
% saying all of the people	59	45	54	5

Source: Data from the 1968 SRC survey.

differences between party identifiers on the race relations issues, with the Democrats somewhat more likely to support government efforts to promote black job equality and school integration. Republicans and Independents are more likely to agree that civil rights groups are pushing too fast. However, a good majority in each of the three identification categories takes that position. With respect to the four other issue areas, differences between Democratic and Republican identifiers are almost nonexistent.

The fact that opinions are more closely divided by party on traditional economic welfare issues than on other issues is not unexpected. The party system that has been in operation for the past few decades was formed in response to Roosevelt, the New Deal, and particularly around the issues of social welfare and regulation of industry and the economy. The leaders of the Democratic party have been more apt to support the development and extension of welfare state type programs, and the party has drawn the bulk of its support from groups that have tended to support such programs. The leadership of the Republican party, on the other hand, has been less likely to initiate and support such measures. Republican supporters over the past several decades have tended to come from social and economic groups that have been more conservative on welfare state issues. These findings, thus, are congruent with both the base of party support and issue positions of the immediate past.

It has been largely around the issues of economic security and industrial regulation that Democratic and Republican party leaders have been able to hold their supporters together and to do electoral battle over the past few decades. It is interesting to note that the extent to which party identification has structured differences in opinion on economic welfare type issues has increased during the 1960s over what it was in the 1950s. For example, the gamma coefficients measuring the level of association between party identification and opinion on the medical assistance proposition were .24 in 1956 and .23 in 1960. In 1964 the coefficient went up to .45, and in 1968 it was .40. The same pattern is evident with respect to the job and standard of living guarantee item. The strength of association with respect to economic welfare issues and party identification went up in 1964 and remains high in 1968, just at the point where the level of association between that issue and both income and political efficacy decrease. (See Tables 4.6 and 6.1.)

Other indicators of the relationships between party identification and these issues suggest the same pattern over time. We would surmise that the change in 1964 and subsequent years resulted from the impact of the Goldwater candidacy in 1964. Among other things, the election that year seems to have resulted in some marginal adjustments between party identification and issue positions, with those with conservative positions on social welfare issues moving more toward the Republican party and those with more liberal outlooks moving more toward the Democratic party. If our assumptions about the relative decrease in the political and electoral saliency of the traditional economic welfare and industrial regulations issues are correct, it would seem that party supporters have become more alike or consistent in their outlooks on welfare state issues at the point when these issues have become less important or relevant in the political arena.

The pattern of relationship over time with respect to the traditional foreign affairs issues is different. The lack of association between party identification and opinions on the isolationism and foreign aid items is constant from 1956 through 1968. International affairs issues have not tended to divide the mass party supporters from each other. Key suggests, on the basis of 1952 and 1956 SRC data, that foreign affairs issues were less important than were domestic issues in determining presidential voting choices.

Among the newer type issues—race relations, Vietnam, public order, and governmental trust—it is only in the area of race relations that party identification is very closely associated with differences of opinion. In the other newer areas of salient political conflict, patterns of party attachment do not relate systematically to differences of opinion. The identifiers of both parties are split on most of these issues, and they are split in proportions generally similar to the divisions within the sample as a whole. Even on the race questions the differences between Democrats, Republicans, and Independents are not as great as those on the economic welfare type issues.

This tendency for differences of opinion on the newer issues to cut through the identifiers of both parties is one of the factors that has made it difficult for the parties to articulate forthright positions on these issues and to provide the electorate with clear alternatives. This has certainly been the case with the Vietnam involvement. It is becoming increasingly the case with some aspects of the contemporary race issue. Party leaders and political candidates are likely to play down and to avoid taking strong, clear stands on issues over which their basic support is divided. Because of such *intraparty* divisions in the 1968 presidential election neither the Democratic nor Republican party, neither Nixon nor Humphrey, was in a good position to offer clear and forthright stands on the issues of Vietnam or race, despite the fact that much of the electorate was very much concerned about these issues. As Lubell pointed out in his analysis "The Revolt of the Voters," this lack of clarity on the part of the major party candidates was an important contributor to voter dissatisfaction in 1968.[4]

Since issues pertaining to race and Vietnam have served as major foci of political attention and their impact is likely to be felt for some time, a more extensive discussion of how parties and elections have related to these particular issues would be useful. They are issues which the parties and electoral processes will be pressed to cope with in one way or another over the next few years. They are also issues which create severe tensions and stress for the existing party coalitions and the social structure of electoral support.

As was pointed out in Chapter 3, the problems surrounding race relations, particularly questions pertaining to the role of the federal government in promoting equality and integration, have emerged over the past two decades as some of the most salient areas of social and political conflict. They are also among the most difficult problems to resolve. Race-related issues have created deep divisions which nearly two decades of attention, discussion, and governmental effort have not resolved or muted. As the discussion in the three preceding chapters points out, the question of government efforts directed toward integration of the public schools has created a fairly even division of opinion within the American public—a division that seems to cut across social-economic lines, age groupings, geographic regions, and variations in political participation and involvement. Only race itself seems to structure opinions on racial policies to any significant degree. As the data in Table 7.1 indicate, differences of opinion on racial questions follow party lines more closely than most of the other social, demographic, and political divisions. Democratic identifiers are somewhat more likely to support civil rights efforts and to be responsive to government efforts to promote integration and equality than are Republicans. These differences between the supporters of the two parties with respect to racial questions have become greater over the past decade. Opinion differences on the black job equality issue and school integration were not structured by differences in party identification prior to 1964. Democrats and Republicans in equal proportions supported and opposed these policies. As with the more traditional economic welfare issues, the 1964 election period seems to be a point of significant shift. Since the Goldwater-Johnson race those who oppose civil rights efforts have become more likely than before to identify with the Republican party, and vice versa. In 1968 slightly more than half of the Democratic identifiers approved of federal efforts directed toward black job equality and school integration. Only about a third of the Republicans took those positions. The opinion distributions among those calling themselves Independents were similar to those of Republican identifiers in 1968.

What do these distributions mean for the important question of how the parties and the electoral system will respond to, or cope with, the contemporary problems of race? Are the parties in the immediate future likely to play up issues relative to race and to offer forthright policies, or to subdue racial concerns and avoid clear issue stands? How effective is the electoral system likely to be in advancing racial equality and integration over the next few years?

We would predict that race policy is one area which the contemporary parties and electoral system will find it very difficult to respond to effectively over the next few years. Major party candidates are less likely to stress racial issues today, and in the immediate future, than they were early in the last decade. There are differences in the extent of party support for racial policies between the two parties, indicating that the parties have somewhat different constituencies with respect to racial questions. The differences are not very great, however. When whites alone are taken into consideration the differences between Democrats and Republicans on school integration and black job equality are substantially diminished. The blacks are very heavily concentrated in the Democratic party. In the 1968 SRC survey 87 percent of the blacks identified themselves as either strong or weak Democrats. When the blacks are not included among those calling themselves Democrats, the percentage of support for the school integration proposition decreases from 51 percent to 41 percent. Similarly the percentage of support for the job equality proposition goes from 52 percent to 42 percent when only white Democrats are considered. The removal of blacks from the sample makes no change among Republican identifiers; 35 percent of the Republicans responded favorably. This indicates that a good portion of the differences between Republicans and Democrats on the racial policy questions results from the heavy concentration of blacks, who, as we pointed out before, have almost unanimous outlooks on these issues, among the Democratic identifiers.

Controversies over race issues have created particularly acute problems for the Democratic party. Race questions divide the basic coalition that constitutes the basic support for the Democratic party more deeply and extensively than any other contemporary issue. On the one hand, blacks and white liberals who strongly favor more government effort directed toward racial equality and integration are very heavily concentrated in the Democratic party and constitute an important component of Democratic electoral support. On the other hand, segments of the population that have become hostile to the substance and the techniques of civil rights efforts also constitute important elements in Democratic support. This latter category includes not only southerners but also increasingly large numbers of "ethnics," manual workers, and union members, all of whom have long constituted major segments of Democratic electoral support. The extent to which various components of the Democratic party are divided on race issues can be appreciated by looking at variations in the level of support for school integration efforts among various types of Democratic identifiers. Ninety percent of those Democratic identifiers who are black responded favorably to the school integration proposition in 1968. Only 41 percent of the white Democratic supporters agreed with the proposition. Among Democrats whose family head's occupation was professional 70 percent supported the proposition. Among Democrats whose family head was a skilled manual worker, only 35 percent supported the school integration proposition. Over the past few years Democratic identifiers on both sides of racial issues have become more concerned and agitated about racial policies.

Some segments of traditional Democratic support have become increasingly resistant to steps taken to bring about racial equality and integration. Other segments of Democratic supporters have intensified their demands and pressures for faster and more extensive efforts. The increasing polarization, coupled with growing intensity of opinion among those groups making up the Democratic party, renders it difficult for the Democratic party to propose and push clear and effective policies with regard to race relations, especially policies involving government action direction toward achieving racial equality and integration. The Democrats are in a "damned if we do, damned if we don't" position on race.

The identifiers with the Republicans party are less evenly divided than the Democrats. Since 1964 persons identifying with the Republican party have been less likely than Democrats to support government civil rights efforts. The Republican party now has relatively few identifiers who strongly and actively pressure for extensive government efforts in the area of race relations. Because few blacks and aggressive civil rights activists are to be found in the Republican party today, the Republicans do not have quite the same dilemma as the Democratic party with respect to civil rights efforts. Nevertheless, racial questions continue to divide Republicans. The debate during the late 1950s and early 1960s over whether the Republicans should make major appeals to blacks in order to carry the northern urban states or to white southerners in order to woo the South away from the Democratic party is an indicator of both the division that existed within the party over race relations questions and the important place of race in the consideration of overall political strategy. More recently the argument over the existence of a "Southern strategy" for the Republican party and intraparty leadership differences regarding school desegregation policy, voting rights legislation, and the attempted appointments of Haynesworth and Carswell to the Supreme Court also testifies to the extent to which race questions can still divide Republicans. Although the national Republican party is less deeply divided over race questions and does not stand to lose as much as the Democrats in terms of party unity and the stability of electoral support, Republicans also are likely to shy away from wanting racial issues to serve as major issues in electoral battles.[5] The Republican party, in particular, is not likely to advocate increased strong efforts with respect to government-forced integration.

One other segment of the electorate must be taken into consideration when dealing with party response to race issues—that is, the Independents, an increasingly large segment of the electorate. As the data in Table 7.1 indicate, the opinion distributions of Independents are rather close to those of Republicans, somewhat more likely to oppose rather than to support government efforts directed toward integration and racial equality. They are even more likely than the Republicans to think that civil rights advocates have been pushing too fast. This factor offers additional testimony to how difficult it will be for the major parties or major party candidates to push strongly and forthrightly increased government efforts directed toward the enforcement of racial integration. If independents are considered as voters or potential voters that can be won by either party, these data suggest that more new votes are to be lost than won by advocating increased government efforts in civil rights.

These various opinion distributions suggest that the current parties and electoral system are not likely to offer forthright, clear, and forceful positions with respect to racial issues. Large segments of the electorate who are greatly agitated about racial problems are likely to be frustrated by the lack of clear responses. Those who want to push forward with even greater efforts directed toward eliminating racial segregation and inequality are not likely to find an enthusiastic response, even by many in the Democratic party. Those who wish to bring a halt to the movement toward racial integration also are likely to find that neither of the major parties wholeheartedly supports that position.

This situation, of course, presents openings for third and fourth parties to exploit the race issue. This was what happened in 1968 with respect to George Wallace and the American Independent Party. Although his appeal and his candidacy were not based exclusively on race, the race issue and a variety of fears associated with it were basic to the Wallace movement. Wallace, of course, appealed to those voters who thought that government efforts directed toward racial integration and equality had gone too far and that civil rights efforts were pushing too fast. Wallace, arguing that there were no differences between the positions of the Democrats and Republicans, appealed to many of those who were frustrated because neither party responded to their fears and concerns.

Since 1968 there has been occasional talk about the formation of a new party on the opposite side of the spectrum from George Wallace. Some blacks and others who are particularly interested in pushing programs designed to aid disadvantaged minorities and to promote equality and integration, among other things, have talked about forming a party more decidedly on the left if the Democrats do not prove more responsive and forthright with respect to racial issues. Whether or not such a party develops and how much appeal it would have remain to be seen. Nevertheless the continued existence of Wallacites and fourth party threats from those on the left do indicate the amount of dissatisfaction with the responses of the major parties to racial and other contemporary concerns.

This situation presents a particularly troublesome situation for those who wish to move more rapidly and more extensively toward the fulfillment of racial integration and equality. The present party and electoral structure and distributions of opinions with respect to civil rights efforts make it difficult for the existing parties and electoral system to serve as a new vehicle for civil rights efforts. The situation which existed in the late 1950s and early 1960s in which both parties sought to woo civil rights supporters in order to win electoral victories and did not run too great a risk of alienating other aspects of their basic support no longer exists. New efforts to redress racial injustices and to push for racial equality and integration through the traditional party and electoral structures will be very difficult to achieve in the immediate future. A continuation of high-saliency conflict over race with opinion distributions structured as they currently are with respect to race, geography, social-economic position, and party identification will put great pressure on the present party coalitions, especially on the divergent groupings which make up the base of Democratic support.

With respect to the other major area of conflict of the past decade, that pertaining to U.S. involvement in Southeast Asia, both Democratic and Republican party leaders and supporters have been even more similarly divided. The extent to which the Vietnam conflict divided the leaders of both parties is well known. The debates and disruptions at the 1968 Democratic convention testify to the extent and intensity of

172 Public Opinion and Contemporary Disarray

division within the leadership of the Democratic party. The fact that the involvement has existed under and been supported by both Democratic and Republican administrations indicates that important elements in both parties have given strong support to the war. The titles of antiwar proposals voted on in the Senate (e.g., Cooper-Church and Hatfield-McGovern) and the fact that votes on the bills split both parties suggest the existence of elements opposed to the war among the representative leadership of both parties.

The public opinion data in Table 7.1 on the three different items eliciting opinions on Vietnam indicate that conflict over the involvement has cut through party support even more than the race policies discussed above. Those data indicate that in 1968 Democratic identifiers thought the involvement was a mistake, favored escalation, and leaned toward support for military victory in almost exactly the same proportions as Republicans. Independents were slightly less likely to think the involvement had been a mistake and to support hawkish positions than either Republican or Democratic identifiers, but the differences were very slight. As we have suggested previously, the fact that the Vietnam war was a particularly salient issue to much of the public in 1968, the fact that the public was fairly evenly divided on a hawk-dove continuum, and the fact that the identifiers of both parties were divided in patterns mirroring the divisions within the entire population combined to make it difficult for the parties and national candidates to respond very effectively to the Vietnam issue. Neither Nixon nor Humphrey was in a position in which either clearly stood to gain more support than he could lose by taking strong, clear stands on the Vietnam conflict. Nixon and the Republicans were likely to gain the most by criticizing the handling of the war by the Johnson administration, promising to handle it better, and pledging to bring it to an honorable end, without being specific as to just what that would entail. Humphrey, on the other hand, was confronted with the more frustrating problem of having to convince the doves in his party that he was not really a hawk on the war, and, at the same time, persuading the hawks that he had not abandoned support of the war and sold out on the Johnson administration. Nixon, of course, had the easier task and was probably more successful on that issue. However, the position of neither candidate nor party was conducive to making the Vietnam involvement the central feature of the campaign or a means through which the voters could clearly express their position on the conflict.

Responses to similar SRC items asked in the 1970 survey suggest both that the population as a whole had moved toward greater opposition to the involvement and away from a hard line or hawkish position, and that Democrats, Republicans, and Independents had all moved in the same direction at roughly the same rate. Support for escalation in response to the item asking what we should do now in Vietnam dropped from 33 percent to 25 percent among Democratic identifiers, from 35 percent to 28 percent among Republican identifiers, and from 42 percent to 30 percent among Independents between 1968 and 1970. Differences between party identifiers had remained very slight. A series of Gallup polls, asking whether persons thought the involvement in the Vietnam conflict had been a mistake, suggest the stability in these interparty similarities from the beginning of the escalation of the conflict in 1965 to the early 1970s. In Chapter 2 (Figure 2.5), we showed the trends from 1965 to 1971 in the proportion of people responding that they thought the involvement had been a mistake. In Figure 7.1 we plot over the same period of time the changes in level of negative judgments regarding that involvement among Democratic and Republican identifiers. The data, again, suggest

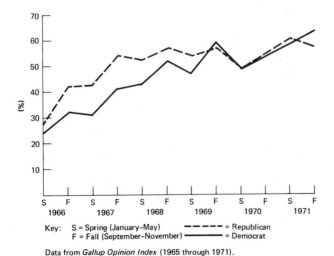

Key: S = Spring (January–May)   – – – – = Republican
      F = Fall (September–November) ——— = Democrat

Data from *Gallup Opinion Index* (1965 through 1971).

FIGURE 7.1.   Percent of the opinion that Vietnam was a mistake (by party I.D.), 1966–1971

that the percentage of people feeling that the involvement had been a mistake had increased substantially from 1965 to 1971 and that Democrats and Republicans moved in the same direction at approximately the same pace. While the percentage of respondents in the entire sample saying the involvement had been a mistake increased from 27 percent in 1966 to 61 percent in 1971, the change among Democrats was from 24 percent to 64 percent and that among Republicans from 27 percent to 58 percent. The greatest disparity in the rate of opposition between the two sets of identifiers was in mid-1967. Republican opposition to the war developed somewhat sooner than that of Democrats, but the Democrats soon caught up.

On these two major conflict areas in contemporary American politics, then, Republican and Democratic identifiers appear not to have been very divergent in their outlooks. More important, the identifiers with both parties have been deeply divided on these issues in ways that make it difficult for the parties to develop and articulate clear, forthright stands. Many voters, who have been very much concerned about the issues of race and the military involvement in Vietnam and who have looked toward the political parties and political leaders to respond to these concerns and provide them with policy proposals, have been left frustrated. The intense feelings of the electorate, the strange new patterns of both divisions within groups and conflicts between groups on these issues, and the ways in which these two factors interact with both political parties have made it particularly difficult for parties and political leaders to respond at just that point in which the citizenry seems to desire clear and meaningful responses.

Party identification appears equally weak in structuring opinion differences on a variety of other issues that have become important in recent years. Data presented in Table 7.1 with respect to public order issues, such as how urban riots should be handled and approval of demonstrations, and the three governmental response and trust items report almost no differences between Democrats and Republicans in response distributions. The responses of Democrats, Republicans, and Independents on a few additional issues of contemporary concern are presented in Table 7.2. Of the issue questions listed in the table party identification is significantly related to opinion distributions only on two issues: the question of how the government should respond to

TABLE 7.2 Party identification and opinions on selected issues, 1969–1970

Issue	Democrats	Independents	Republicans	Difference between Democrats and Republicans
Government and Pollution * % favoring government regulation	72%	79%	71%	1%
Rights of Accused* % saying do anything necessary to stop crime	45	51	53	8
Student Demonstrations* % leaning toward use of force	59	70	75	16
Urban riots* % leaning toward use of force	29	34	36	7
Government Health Insurance % leaning toward government program	56	42	30	26
Defense Spending[a] % saying too much spent	49	55	53	4
Price and Wage Controls[b] % favoring	54	50	58	4

Source: *Data from 1970 SRC election survey.
[a] Gallup Poll, AIPO 784, July, 1969.
[b] Gallup Poll, AIPO 783, June 1969, Question 7.

student demonstrators, and the proposition regarding a general health insurance program. Democrats are less likely than Republicans and Independents to lean toward the use of force in responding to student demonstrations, though sentiment among Democrats is skewed in that direction, too. By 26 percentage points Democrats lean more toward favoring a program of government health insurance, though even among Democrats there is no overwhelming consensus in support of the idea. The relationship with respect to the health insurance issue offers further confirmation for the point discussed above. It is primarily on economic welfare type issues that Democrats and Republicans have the most divergent opinions. If our assumptions about the shift in issue focus and saliency are correct (see the discussion in the first half of Chapter 3), the parties are most extensively differentiated from each other with respect to an issue area which has become less important to much of the electorate.

The relationships between parties, voting, and opinion distributions become even clearer when one considers how issue opinions are distributed among different voter types in the 1968 presidential election. Table 7.3 compares opinions on the major issues from the 1968 survey among Humphrey (Democratic), Nixon (Republican), and Wallace (American Independent) voters, and nonvoters. As was the case with party identification, Democratic and Republican voters are most clearly differentiated by opinions on economic welfare type issues, especially the medical assistance questions. Race relations questions divide the Humphrey and Nixon voters only slightly less. Differences between Democratic and Republican voters on the remainder of the 1968 issue items are relatively less, though some-what greater with respect to the question on how to deal with urban riots than for any of the other issues.

Wallace voters have opinion distributions which clearly distinguish them from Democratic voters, Republican voters, and nonvoters on almost every issue. Those who reported having voted for Wallace were decidedly less likely than all of the other voting groupings to support government civil rights efforts. They were almost unanimous in opposition to the school integration proposition and in thinking that civil rights had been pushed too fast. They decidedly favored a tougher position in Vietnam, opposed demonstrations, and favored the use of

TABLE 7.3 Vote for president and opinions on issues, 1968

Issue	Humphrey	Nixon	Wallace	Nonvote
Government Medical Assistance % in favor	76%	41	57	76
Government Job and Living Guarantee % in favor	46	22	29	44
Government Too Powerful % saying "Yes"	34	68	77	54
Government Promote Black Job Equality % for	58	35	25	47
Government Promote School Integration % for	62	38	7	41
Civil Rights Pushing Too Fast % agreeing	51	69	90	64
Foreign Aid % for	54	46	29	43
Vietnam Involvement a Mistake % saying a mistake	43	37	31	33
What Do Now in Vietnam? % for escalation	27	37	62	33
Attitude on Vietnam % leaning military victory	32	42	65	39
Urban Riots % leaning toward use of force	16	33	66	31
Demonstrations % expressing disapproval	46	54	71	56
Government Listen to People % great deal of time	32	26	11	19
Government Trusted to Do Right % trusting all or most of the time	72	63	40	60

Source: Data from 1968 SRC survey.

force in dealing with urban riots. They also trusted the government less and were less likely to see the government as responding to people. The strong opposition to civil rights efforts, get-tough stance on riots and demonstrations, and support for escalation of the war coupled with considerably more disaffection from government are additional evidence that in 1968 disaffection and discontent with the government and the thrust of American politics were concentrated more on the "right" of the contemporary political spectrum than on the "left." On the medical assistance question and the job and standard of living issue Wallace voters fell in between the Humphrey and Nixon voters. They were more likely to support government efforts in these two fields than were Nixon voters, but less supportive than Humphrey voters.

It is also important to note how nonvoters compare to Democratic and Republican voters on the various issues. With respect to both the medical assistance and the job and standard of living issues nonvoters indicated levels of support almost exactly equal to that of the Humphrey voters. On almost every other issue, however, the opinions of the nonvoters were closest to those of the Republicans. The only exceptions to this were the black job equality item and what do do now in Vietnam question on which nonvoters fell almost exactly in between Democratic and Republican voters. On the other two race relations issues and the public order type issues the nonvoters had opinion distributions very similar to those of Republicans.

If one can assume that issues, especially salient issues, influence voting choices and that 1968 Wallace voters and nonvoters are potential sources of new votes, the comparisons between Wallace voters, nonvoters, and Humphrey and Nixon voters take on particular importance in making speculations concerning party strategies and prospects. These relationships, together with the relationships between party identification and issue preferences, indicate that the Democrats are most likely to pick up additional support among nonvoters and Wallace voters on the basis of traditional economic welfare type issues. Likewise it is on economic welfare type issues that Democrats are likely to maximize support among their own supporters and identifiers. Given the fact that the Democratic party is the majority party (the party with the largest number of identifiers), by a wide margin, the maintenance of support that the party already has is generally the most important electoral objective. That is, one of the main tasks for the Democrats for the winning of national elections today is selecting candidates and stressing issues that allow them to hold onto those persons who already identify with the party, and to interest them in the election and get them out to vote. The changes in issue emphasis and the fact that issue conflicts increasingly cut across important social groupings make this task difficult for the Democratic party today.

Issues other than the traditional economic welfare type issues are more likely to split mass Democratic support rather than hold them together. For example, taking a strong, forthright stand in favor of increased government pressure for racial integration—forced bussing to bring about school desegregation, for example—may appeal to some black Democrats and to those white Democrats who very strongly support racial integration. At the same time such a stand would tend to alienate many of the white Democrats who are not enthusiastic about such objectives, and in some instances are strongly opposed to them. On the other hand, taking a position in favor of slowing down, or turning back, the thrust toward racial equality and integration would risk the possibility of losing support among blacks and other civil rights liberals, even though it might make other segments of the party happier. The same potential has existed with respect to the issue of Vietnam and some types of public order issues. The establishment of strong intraparty consensus on issues other than the traditional economic welfare concerns is probably the crucial issue facing the Democratic party today.

The same conditions of new issue conflicts which cut through the population in patterns different from the traditional economic issues create problems for the Republican party as well. The dilemmas, however, are probably not as great. As the minority party, change and flux offer potential advantages for the Republicans as well as disadvantages. First, the Democratic party is the party whose supporters and general outlook have corresponded most closely to the general consensus on economic welfare type issues. The majority Democratic coalition was built around support for the New Deal economic welfare and industrial regulation programs. As the 1964 election indicated, the Republican party does not stand much of a chance to win by seriously opposing such programs, even if many of its leaders and identifiers tend to be against them. The Republican party, unlike the Democratic party, does not stand to gain by keeping traditional economic issues as the central focus of elections and political discussion. Second, the minority party can potentially pick up new support from dissonant elements within the majority party. Thus, the disarray and internal divisions within the Democratic party can work to the advantage of the Republicans, depending, of course, on whether or not they are in a position to exploit them. Third, as the data in Table 7.3 suggest the opinion distributions among Republicans on most of the newer type issues are more like those of the Wallace voters and the nonvoters than those among the Democrats. Potentially then, the Republican party appears to be in a better position to gain from the newer type issues.

The situation, however, is not so clear-cut nor so rosy for the Republicans. Although not as severely divided as the Democratic party on most of the newer issues, there have been significant divisions within the Republican party—particularly on race and Vietnam. These internal divisions, as well as the overall divisions in the society at large, which do not offer a clear majority position toward which either party can move, continue to circumscribe the policy positions of the Republicans.

In this chapter we have attempted to show how the various issue conflicts interact with existing party and electoral structures. We have suggested that for the most part the newer type issues cut through the basic party and voting coalitions rather than being structured by them and that this factor has contributed to the difficulty which the parties and political leaders have had in responding to current political concerns and demands. The combination of new issues, high levels of conflict, divisions which cut across many of the social economic groupings that have been particularly relevant politically, and intraparty divisions combine to make it very difficult for the electoral and the political structures to deal very effectively with contemporary political problems and issues.

Notes

[1] The major exceptions to this were conflicts within the Democratic party during the first few decades of the twentieth century concerning whether or not the national party should come out against the Ku Klux Klan and attempt to pass federal antilynching legislation.

[2] A number of factors including the division of powers within the American political system, the local focus of many political contests, and the diverse makeup of American political parties could be mentioned in this regard.

[3] Through the use of a series of questions The Survey Research Center in its political surveys has developed a seven-position party identification index: Strong Democrat, Weak Democrat, Independent Democrat, Independent, Independent Republican, Weak Republican, and Strong Republican.

[4] Samuel Lubell, *The Hidden Crisis in American Politics* (New York: Norton, 1970), pp. 55-56.

[5] Nixon, of course, has come out very strongly in opposition to the use of bussing to bring about forceful integration of schools. We would guess that this move

was made primarily to counteract the potential impact of George Wallace and a Wallacite third party movement. It is quite likely that if there was not the possibility of such a third party that could play up the bussing issue, Nixon would not have taken such a strong public position.

CHAPTER 8
CONCLUSIONS: POLITICAL OPINIONS AND CONTEMPORARY POLITICS

At the outset of this discussion we asserted that the disquiet, disarray, and confusion in contemporary American political life could be understood, in part, by an investigation of the content and distribution of mass opinions on political and social issues. In this chapter we review and pull together the various facets of issue saliency and opinion distributions presented in the preceding chapters and speculate on the implications of these factors for American politics now and in the immediate future. What are the consequences of changes in issue focus, the altered structuring of political conflict and consensus, and the disintegration of political coalitions for the future of American political life?

We have argued that over the past decade several new major types of political and social issues have emerged as salient political concerns for many Americans. At the same time concern with and contention over more traditional policies involving economic security and industrial regulation seem to have waned. The major new issue areas we have identified are race relations, Vietnam or the American military involvement in Southeast Asia, and public order. Each of these broad areas entails a number of more particular issues which have served as particular policy conflicts—for example, job quotas for minorities and the use of bussing to force integration in public schools, the use of massive bombing to force a settlement in the Vietnam conflict and the level of spending for national defense, the use of wiretapping and tougher penalties as means of combating crime, and the legalization of abortions to terminate pregnancies.

The often intense conflicts that have surrounded these new issues and the difficulties that government and political leaders have had in responding to them have contributed to an additional major area of concern and controversy, that of governmental trust and responsiveness. Over the past few years questions pertaining to the candor of public officials, controversies as to who the government is and to whom government should be responsive, and even more fundamental questioning of whether or not the existing "political system" can cope with current social and political problems have become points of political contention. While some people have been pushing for significant changes in basic political institutions and procedures, other have clung even more tenaciously to the traditional arrangements. Popular concepts such as "credibility gap," the "quality of life," the "reordering of national priorities," the "environmental crisis," "liberation" for women and blacks, "neoisolationism," "antiestablishment," and "middle America" testify both to the shifts in political concerns and the questioning of political processes.

Several significant points regarding these new issue areas and their impact on contemporary Americans politics should be reiterated and stressed at this point. First, these new issues are concurrently questions about which there is great popular concern and issues which deeply divide the American people. Intense and divisive political conflicts have developed around these issues. The sense of consensus and the belief that economic abundance and growth would provide the basis for solving social and economic problems (ideas which were prominent in the mid-1960s), have been followed by polarization, intensified conflict, and a feeling of political futility.

Second, each of these new areas of political concern—race, Vietnam, public order, and governmental trust—represents social, economic, political, and moral problems for which there are not easy and quick solutions. Even the cease-fire in Vietnam is not likely to bring to an end some of the intense moral and political conflicts that have developed with respect to that involvement. In addition to their consequences for the economic well-being and the power positions of groups and individuals, these new areas of contention often have important implications for personal morals and prejudices, for deeply ingrained political and social values, and for the images people have of their country and its position in the world. The promotion of racial equality may mean enhancing the economic positions of blacks, but it also constitutes a challenge to deeply ingrained notions of racial differences. The use of minority quotas in hiring and representation, the legalization of marijuana and abortion, and the "liberation" of women constitute for many people challenges to their "sense of justice," their ideas concerning "correct behavior," and their notions of "the proper order of things." The decrease of expenditures for the military could have economic consequences. It could make more money available for other areas of governmental expenditures. However, it also is viewed as a threat to the power position of the United States vis-à-vis other nations and as possibly undermining the role of the United States as world policeman. A guaranteed family income maintenance program may be an economically feasible way to cope with the problem of persistent poverty in the midst of general affluence. It is also seen by many as a challenge to the notion that one should be rewarded according to his labor. This notion is an important component of the economic and social creeds of many Americans.

The point is that these issues have moral and social value implications that take precedence over economic considerations in the outlooks of many Americans. As such they may prove less susceptible, than were issues of economic security and industrial regulation, to the techniques of incrementalism, group bargaining, and compromise— methods that have played an important part in American politics. The issues and conflicts that have surrounded the problem of race relations, the question of American involvement in Vietnam, and the many facets of public order and governmental trust are likely to confront American politics and to frustrate political leadership for some time to come.

A third important point about contemporary issue conflicts is that no single issue or issue area clearly dominates the contemporary scene. No one issue area seems to remain the most pressing political concern for most of the public over very long spans of time. For many the Vietnam conflict has been the paramount issue. For others it has been race relations. For still others crime and public order constitute the number one political and social concerns. For yet others the state of the economy or the honesty and effectiveness of government has been the most salient political concern. Even for the same people the relative saliency of these several areas tends to change over short time spans. Changes often occur in response to the most recent event. A racial

disturbance or a school desegregation decision, an escalation or
de-escalation of military activity in Vietnam, riots or demonstrations on
a college campus, a sharp rise in the cost of living, or a report indicating
a rise in the crime rate can quickly alter the chief issue concerns of large
segments of the public.

The point is that none of these several major issue areas has achieved
the position of the dominant concern on the political agenda. Nor are
opinions in the various issue areas always closely related to each other
within the public. The lack of dominant issue focus was evident in the
1972 presidential campaign. The leaders of both major parties seemed
to agree that issues should be stressed in the election and that the two
candidates offered unusually clear alternatives with respect to major
national policies. One candidate referred to the campaign as the clearest
policy choice in this century. Party leaders, however, seemed unsure as
to just which issues were most important to the bulk of the electorate.
Different spokesmen, at different times, variously stressed the Vietnam
conflict, the state of the economy, the trust and credibility of
government, crime and public order, tax reform and defense
expenditures as the central issue of the day. Throughout the campaign
there was little clarity as to which of several issues was most salient to
most of the public, let alone any clear assessment as to which party had
the advantage with respect to which issues. Not only was it unclear with
the respect to the Vietnam issue whether more voters were likely to be
impressed by the picture of continued involvement and escalation of
the bombing stressed by the Democrats or by the picture of the
substantial withdrawal of ground combat troops pushed by the
Republicans; it was not clear how important the whole issue of
Vietnam was likely to be in determining electoral choices. How salient
the issue of defense spending was in comparison to other issues was as
unclear as the question of whether more votes were to be won by
pledging substantial cuts in defense appropriations or in pledging to
maintain high expenditures to keep America number one in military
power. There is evidence that race relations was one of the most
important underlying issues in the minds of many voters. Yet, neither
of the candidates played up racial issues in the fall campaign.

If we have been correct in our assumptions concerning the relatively
high level of concern and involvement with issues on the part of the

public and in our assessment about the shift in issue focus, the contemporary situation is one of high, but diffuse and volatile, issue focus. This factor, coupled with the tendency for opinion distributions on these various issues not to be too strongly interrelated (see the second part of Chapter 3), has made it particularly difficult for political leaders to build enduring issue coalitions and to focus attention on the solution of particular problems.

The bulk of our analysis has focused on how political opinions in the contemporary period are structured by various economic, social, political, and demographic conditions. We have discussed, in some detail, the extent to which differences in political outlooks are related to variations in occupation and income, regional location, race, age, religious identification, level of political participation and involvement, and political party attachment. We have pointed out that important shifts have taken place over time in the impact of some of these factors in structuring political conflict and consensus. These shifts are an important component of the current political disarray. They contribute to the sense of frustration. They have important consequences for the structure of American political life in the immediate future.

These changes suggest a sort of "destructuring"[1] of basic patterns of conflict and consensus. Over the past decade conditions such as social-economic position and geography seem to have become less significant in determining political outlooks. It is particularly apparent that cleavages surrounding the newer type issues cut through the population in patterns different from the cleavages centering around the salient welfare state issues of the 1930s, 1940s, and 1950s. For example, opinions regarding the involvement in Vietnam and various aspects of the public order issue have not followed occupational lines as closely as did earlier conflicts over welfare efforts and government regulation of business. We shall review briefly the basic findings concerning the structural distribution of opinions and then discuss more explicitly how these patterns, or shifts from earlier patterns, contribute to the contemporary political disarray and make difficult the task of effective political response.

Among the most significant of the changes we have noted is that social-economic position has come to play a relatively less important role in the structuring of opinion differences. Political preferences on most issues in the present period are less closely associated with differences in occupation and level of family income than they were during the period running from the Depression of the 1930s, through World War II, and the decade or so following that war. In Chapter 4 we presented several types of evidence indicating that the relationship between social-economic position and political opinions had been substantially weakened by the early 1960s. First, using a time series of items asking about preferences on welfare and industrial regulation items, running from the mid-1930s through the mid-1960s, we found that occupation and income structured differences of opinions on these types of issues to a considerable degree up to the mid-1950s. By the early 1960s, however, differences in opinions with respect to questions such as the level of spending for welfare, the role of the government in providing medical assistance, and the amount of government regulation of business were not very closely related to differences in occupation and income level. The clear cut divisions between economic groupings with respect to welfare state issues had disappeared. This trend seems to have continued over the past decade. Even in instances where there is substantial disagreement over policies within the population as a whole, the divisions tend to cut through social-economic groupings. Where differences between occupational groupings exist, the divisions tend not to follow very clearly the traditional pattern of clear distinctions between manual workers and nonmanual workers. In some instances the opinion distributions of skilled manual workers have come to look much more similar to those of white-collar workers and less like those of other types of manual workers.

In addition to the decreasing role of social economic position in structuring outlooks on welfare state issues, we have found that, for the most part, opinions on the newer type issues are not closely related to occupation and income, at least not in any orderly, systematic fashion. Opposition to the Vietnam involvement has not come disproportionately from those at either the bottom or the top of the occupational and income hierarchies. Professionals at the top and nonskilled workers at the bottom have been the two occupational groupings most likely to favor government efforts to promote racial integration and equality. Skilled workers and farmers have been somewhat more likely than those in other occupations to oppose such efforts.

The existence of significant areas of salient policy and issue conflicts which are not structured by social-economic position constitutes a significant development in American political life. Although there have always been important exceptions (e.g., regional and religious-ethnic variations), electoral coalitions, patterns of partisan support, and preferences on domestic welfare issues have tended to follow social-economic lines since the early days of the New Deal. The "have-not's" have been concentrated in the Democratic party. They have tended to support liberal Democratic candidates and to back social welfare programs. The wealthier citizens have tended to support the Republican party and to be less enthusiastic about government welfare and industrial regulation efforts.

Not only has social-economic position tended to structure voting and political choices, it has been an important perceptual factor as well. The assumption that political outlooks are associated with social-economic position has been a major component in the way we have looked at political behavior. The Democratic party has been known popularly as the party of the working man. The Republican party generally has been known as the party of business and the wealthy. Parties and political leaders have tended to support or oppose programs and to select candidates with some fairly clear expectations as to whether or not they would appeal to one income or occupational grouping or another. Candidates running for office have based campaign strategies on assumptions that they should attempt to mobilize voters in some economic groupings, and not those in others. Social science theories regarding voting behavior have taken as assumptions the impact of social-economic position in explaining and predicting electoral choices. To a considerable degree we have tended to look at and to "understand" American political behavior as determined and structured in large part by social-economic position.

The waning influence of social-economic position in structuring political divisions and agreements represents the demise of a major ordering component and of significant political reference points. In addition this change means that many of the groups organized around occupational and income categories find themselves with deeply divided constituencies with respect to major national policy issues. Such divisions have become evident over the past few years. Internal divisions concerning contemporary political issues have been particularly evident within organized labor. Among both the leaders and the mass membership there have developed wide differences of opinion with respect to most significant current policy issues. On very few of the salient issues does one find consensus, either within the leadership or the rank and file of the unions. Policies concerning racial equality and integration deeply divide labor, as they do most other segments of the population. Both union leadership and rank-and-file membership have been divided over Vietnam policy. Some union leaders have provided leadership for the opposition to the involvement. Others have served as a bulwark of support for U.S. policy. Contemporary conflicts over how to handle crime and public order, the reduction of spending for defense, the reordering of national priorities, and the state of the environment are not issues that unite either the ranks or the leadership of the labor movement. Even some contemporary welfare policies and proposals for income redistribution, the types of programs which in the past labor has tended to unite behind, do not engender widespread labor support. Proposals for a family income maintenance program and for tax reforms designed to redistribute income drew mixed reactions from organized labor during the 1972 presidential campaign.

The most dramatic example of how these new patterns of opinion divisions have affected the politics and unity of organized labor can be seen in the varied responses of union leadership to the nomination of George McGovern as the Democratic presidential candidate in 1972. Breaking with the pattern of the past few decades, organized labor did not line up strongly behind the Democratic standard bearer. Many prominent labor leaders refused to endorse either McGovern or his Republican opponent, Richard Nixon. This was the position taken by the national labor federation, the AFL–CIO. It was also the stance of some major international unions such as the United Steel Workers. Other unions, such as the Teamsters and some of the building trade unions, supported the reelection of Nixon. Still others, such as the United Auto Workers, remained loyal to the Democratic party. The extent to which the altered patterns of issue focus and conflict affected electoral support was demonstrated in the 1972 election results. Nixon carried the majority of the votes of manual workers in general, as well as those of union members in particular, by slight margins. These same types of intragroup divisions with respect to contemporary political issues exist today within other occupational and economic-oriented groupings and organizations. Business, professional, and white-collar workers have been divided over issues pertaining to racial policy, Vietnam, and public order.

Our analysis also has suggested that other factors that have been presumed to structure opinions in American society do not significantly pattern issue cleavages at the present time. On the major issues of the late 1960s and early 1970s there appears to be little variation in opinion distributions within the major geographic regions. Major contemporary political issues do not pit the North against the South or the East against the West. Even on the race-related questions differences between the South and other sections of the nation are less pronounced now than in earlier decades. Similarly differences in political outlooks on national policy issues between the two major religious groupings seem to be virtually nonexistent in the present period. We interpret these findings as indicating that religious-ethnic identifications, which have been important in structuring political outlooks in the past, also have become less significant in ordering political preferences. The lack of differences between Catholics and Protestants seems to hold both for the more traditional economic welfare type issues and for the new types of political concerns.

If this limited analysis is accurate, it seems that American politics are losing still other traditional ordering and reference points. Social-economic position, regionalism, and religious-ethnic identifications—the three factors that have been most important in structuring American political life—do not seem to be closely associated with the divisions in contemporary politics.

Two other conditions were explored in the preceding discussion, age and race. With respect to age the findings suggest that on major national policy issues opinion distributions between major age groupings are not great. Where differences occur it is generally the older citizens, those fifty and over, who differ from the middle and young groups. This pattern is not consistent with the popular notion of the generation gap which portrays the young, those under thirty, as significantly different in political outlooks from their elders. Despite the lack of significant differences between the young and their elders on the major types of policy issues which we have been considering, it is possible that distribution patterns more in keeping with those suggested by the generation gap notion may exist with respect to some types of issues. Youth, for example, are more likely than their elders to support the legalization of abortions and of marijuana. In 1972 younger voters voted for McGovern in higher proportions than did older voters. Although age may influence opinions in certain areas at this point, it has not become a major factor in structuring conflict over major national political issues.

Race presents a different picture. It was with respect to racial divisions that we found the highest levels of opinion structuring. On nearly every type of issue—social welfare, race, Vietnam, and public order—blacks have opinion distributions that are clearly distinct from those of whites. On race and welfare type issues, there is near unanimity of opinion among blacks. Almost all blacks are liberals on these issues. Opinions among whites are more evenly divided. In Chapters 5 and 7 we discussed some of the implications of racial polarization for political parties, voting, and the future of policies regarding race relations. We argued that the increased intensity and polarization of opinions regarding governmental race policies, the relatively small proportion of blacks in the population, and the growing division within the Democratic party over race-related issues have made it increasingly difficult to deal with the issues of racial equality and integration through the normal electoral and policy-making processes.

With respect to basic social-economic and demographic conditions we have found that contemporary political conflicts are not highly structured by, or related to, those basic social conditions which tended to divide and structure the citizenry in the past. Race, of course, is the major exception. In a manner similar to that suggested by Lane and others who have attempted to analyze and predict the impact of economic affluence and advanced industrialization on political life, many of the economic and demographic conflicts and tensions that provided the structure and the dynamics for much of political life seem to be subsiding.[2] However, contrary to the projections of Lane, the lessening of politically relevant tensions between economic and other groupings has not ushered in an era of political consensus and contentment. Rather, new areas of conflict have arisen—conflicts that do not follow the more traditional lines of social-economic position, geography, and ethnicity.

Relationships between political outlooks and social and demographic groupings are not the only relationships that have been altered over the past few decades. As we pointed out in Chapter 6 and 7, conflicts on many of the newer type issues do not relate very strongly or systematically to partisan identifications and political participation. The identifiers with both major parties and both Democratic and Republican presidential voters in 1968 were divided over issues pertaining to Vietnam, public order, and race. Levels of electoral participation, electoral involvement, and political efficacy seem to have become less strongly associated with political opinions over the past decade, following a pattern very similar to the decreasing relationship between income and occupation and political outlooks. The newer type issues cut through and divide the basic partisan and electoral coalitions that have operated in American politics over the past forty years. Democratic identifiers exhibit intense and opposing views on government race relations policies. Republican identifiers have been divided over Vietnam policies.

The divisions within the political coalitions can also be seen with respect to the social groupings that make up the electoral and partisan groupings. The coalitions of the New Deal party system were formed by bringing together several population groupings that shared common outlooks on the issues of economic security and industrial regulation, which were the central political concerns of that period.[3] Labor unions and industrial workers, blacks, ethnic minorities, and other ideological liberals were brought together under the rubric of the Democratic party. They tended to work and to vote together in support of liberal Democratic candidates and New Deal programs. Business and professional people, old-stock Protestants, and residents of small towns outside the South tended to vote together as Republicans and to oppose liberal welfare state measures.

The newer issues and conflicts of the 1960s and 1970s tend to cut through these group coalitions in two significant ways. First, the blacks, the white industrial workers, and the ethnics in metropolitan areas do not necessarily share common interests and policy preferences with respect to race-related issues. Job quotas, forced integration of schools, and open housing are viewed positively by most blacks. They see them as important steps in their battle for equality and justice. To many white industrial workers and urban ethnics, on the other hand, these policies are viewed as potential threats to their economic security, social status, and sometimes even their sense of justice. The tendency toward racial polarization among groups that have traditionally been united within the Democratic party has become a common pattern within major American cities over the past decade. The pattern has been particularly pronounced in cities such as Newark, New Jersey, Cleveland, Ohio, and Gary, Indiana, which have combinations of large black populations and large numbers of ethnic minorities. For example, voting in the past three elections for mayor in Cleveland has tended to follow racial lines very closely. Black voters have voted very solidly for black Democratic candidates. White ethnic voters have tended to vote only a little less solidly for white Republican candidates. Prior to the mid-1960s both blacks and white ethnics voted together very solidly for Democratic candidates. Professionals appear more likely than skilled manual workers and urban ethnics to side with blacks on issues involving racial integration and equality. With respect to public order issues some union leaders and ethnic associations have been leading proponents of toughness and using all necessary force in handling urban riots. Blacks and middle-class liberals have tended to be more negative about the use of force and to favor dealing with underlying social and economic causes.

The traditional ties between various social groupings and party and electoral coalitions have broken down in another respect as well. It is not only that major social groupings that in the past worked together in the political arena in the pursuit of common goals today have conflicting interests and outlooks. As we pointed out above, the members or identifiers of many groupings are not in agreement among themselves when it comes to some contemporary issues. Not only do unions and white ethnic groups not share common interests and political objectives with blacks and other components of the New Deal Democratic coalition, they do not share common interests and viewpoints among themselves. Businessmen and professionals, have been divided over policies regarding race, Vietnam, public order, and sometimes even welfare type issues. Social, economic, religious-ethnic, and demographic groupings which have been so important in tying individuals into political parties and electoral coalitions are not as relevant as political reference groups under these altered conditions.[4] Blacks, union members, Jews, and white ethnics still tend to identify themselves as Democrats. Under many circumstances they vote together for Democratic candidates. They often have differing outlooks on many political issues. Sometimes, as in the 1972 presidential election, these different interests and preferences lead them to vote differently. Growing tensions have developed among the groups making up the political parties and electoral coalitions. These tensions are particularly acute within the majority Democratic coalition.

The destructuring of political outlooks with respect to the more traditional social, economic, and demographic lines, and the tendency of individual and group constituencies of the parties to have divergent interests and outlooks on salient political issues, contribute to the contemporary disarray and frustration. The changes in issue focus, the increasing saliency of political issues and political conflicts, and the fact that outlooks on salient political concerns are not closely associated either with significant social groupings or with partisan coalitions make it difficult for political leadership to focus on and to respond to contemporary political demands. It does not seem inaccurate to portray the current situation as one in which the basic coalitions and many of the political symbols and relationships, which were developed around one set of political issues and problems, are confronted with new issues and new cleavages for which these traditional relationships and associations are not particularly relevant. Given these conditions, the widespread confusion, frustration, and mistrust are not surprising.

Our argument concerning the distributions of political opinions and how they contribute to the contemporary political climate should be clear by this point. What impact are these factors likely to have on politics in the immediate future? Is the current state of disarray, of conflicts that are not structured either by basic social groupings or by existing partisan coalitions, likely to continue for some time? Can the existing party and electoral systems adjust to and come to grips with these new patterns of division and issue focus? Might we soon develop a new party system, one with electoral alignments that will be more closely related to the new patterns of conflict and agreement? These questions lead to a topic that is currently much discussed in both the popular press and the scholarly literature—that is, the issue of whether or not we are in the midst of a major new political realignment.[5]

Many political analysts and historians have conceptualized the development of American politics as cyclical alterations between periods of general stability in issue focus, in party labels, and in electoral coalitions, on the one hand, and brief periods of abrupt changes in the patterns of political focus and conflict.[6] These fundamental changes have been identified with particular national elections. These elections have been referred to as critical elections. There is general agreement that elections in 1800 when Jefferson was elected president, in 1828 which saw the triumph of the Jacksonian Democrats, in 1860 when Lincoln was elected in the midst of sectional splits in the Democratic and remnants of the Whig parties, the Bryan-McKinley contest in 1896, and the emergence of the New Deal coalitions with the electoral victories of Roosevelt in 1932 and 1936 constituted such important turning points in American politics. They entailed important shifts in the group makeup of parties and in the alignment of the electorate. They accompanied intensified concern over new issues—issues that had divided the existing party coalitions and had created severe tensions within the electoral groupings of the time. More often than not these periods of electoral realignment were preceded by the rise of minor political parties. These minor parties, for at least a short while, were able to represent positions on new issues and to give vent to frustrations which the existing major parties were not responding to.[7] These brief periods of change have been followed by longer periods in which there has been general stability in the patterns of electoral alignment and political concerns established by the realignment. As we have suggested before, the last of these important realignments took place in the 1930s when the New Deal party coalitions were put together.

Our analysis has indicated that severe tensions have emerged within the existing partisan and electoral coalitions. The coalitions which developed around the New Deal and the issues of economic security and industrial regulation are being divided internally by new political concerns and by the breakdown of former issue-group relationships. The issue-oriented divisions and group conflicts within the Democratic party with respect to the 1968 and 1972 elections show quite vividly how these new patterns of issue conflict cut through the majority party coalition. The Democratic primary and convention battles in 1968 and 1972 were not simply battles over leadership ability or personalities, or even between vaguely designated conservative and liberal wings of the party. They were contests between candidates and factions which represented divergent positions on a number of salient issues. The different factions also held different views on the direction the party should take, both ideologically and organizationally.

Having won the nomination in 1972 after a long series of primary and convention battles, McGovern was unable (or unwilling) to develop a campaign, or to articulate issue positions that could hold the divided party coalition together. Nor was he able to put together an effective new coalition based on groups aligned around the newer concerns and demands. The result was a major reelection victory for Richard Nixon, with large numbers of traditionally Democratic voters breaking with the party to vote against their own candidate. There were large defections among some of the major component groups of the Democratic coalition—manual workers, labor unions, white ethnics, Catholics, and Jews. Nixon made a clean sweep of the once solidly Democratic South.

We have suggested at several points that the tendency for contemporary issues to divide rather than to unite the party groupings, as well as many of the politically relevant social and demographic groupings, are major factors contributing to the difficulty that political leadership and the electoral system have in responding to and focusing on issues that are important to many people today. This, in turn, contributes to a key political concern, that of governmental trust and responsiveness. The problems surrounding race, the involvement in Vietnam, and the many facets of public order would be difficult issues for the political system to cope with under the best of circumstances. The combination of difficult problems, new patterns of social and political conflicts, and the tendency for these cleavages not to be related systematically to the conditions that have structured politics in the immediate past, all work together to create the present climate of disarray, frustration, and distrust. If these assessments are correct, the prospects for the establishment of new party and electoral groupings which would center around these new issues and patterns of agreement and disagreement are important considerations.

There are a number of factors that suggest the likelihood of new electoral realignments. Many of the conditions that have accompanied such realignments in the past are present. There has been a significant shift in issue focus and an intensification in policy and issue concerns in the electorate. There is a lack of congruence between distributions of opinions on political issues and basic partisan and electoral coalitions. There has been a proliferation in attempts to influence governmental action outside the normal party and electoral channels—for example, demonstrations, protests, nonparty political movements. In 1968 an important third party contested the presidency, the American Independent Party under the leadership of George Wallace. The large number of votes Wallace received in 1968 and his showing in Democratic primaries in 1972 testify to the discontent and frustration many voters feel with respect to the major parties. In 1968 the appeal of the Wallace American Party centered primarily around race and public order type issues. In appealing to voters in the 1968 election, Wallace argued that there was not a dime's worth of difference between the two major parties. He offered an alternative.

The 1972 national elections have been scrutinized in terms of their indications of a basic party realignment. In the early stages of the campaign Nixon and Republican leaders referred to the building of a new majority. Some liberal Democrats talked about developing a new, more liberal coalition as the base of the Democratic party. The election results themselves are open to different interpretations. On the one hand, the vote for president indicated a major breech in the majority Democratic coalition. Large numbers of traditionally Democratic voters cast ballots for the Republican candidate. Many of them seem to have voted for him because they did not like positions taken by the Democratic candidate—his position on Vietnam, on defense spending, on public order or public morality issues, on racial policies, or on public welfare and tax reform. In this respect the Democratic defections to Nixon are unlike those to Eisenhower in 1952 and 1956. Although not totally devoid of policy meaning, much of Eisenhower's drawing power was based on his personal stature and popularity. This does not appear to have the case with Nixon in 1972. On the other hand, the voting for other national and for state offices can be interpreted to indicate the staying power of the Democratic coalition. Despite the massive landslide victory of the Republican presidential candidate, the Republican party failed to win control of either house of Congress and did not do particularly well in contests for state offices. In fact, the Democrats picked up a net gain of one Senate seat and one governship. They lost only a nominal number of seats in the national House of Representatives.

These mixed results certainly are not conclusive evidence that the Republicans have put together a new and enduring majority coalition. They do, however, offer additional evidence of the internal divisions and tensions within the existing party coalitions. The large amount of split-ticket voting (voting for the candidate of one party for one office and for candidates of the other party for other offices) suggests the weakening of the party ties. The mixed election results and the general issue ambiguity of the campaign also make it difficult to identify clear issue mandates or preferences on the part of the electorate.

Despite the considerable evidence suggesting the divisions within the existing party coalitions and the presence of conditions that in the past have been associated with electoral realignments, a major partisan realignment does not see imminent. Several conditions make the formation of new stable electoral coalitions, or basic electoral realignment, difficult. These factors stem from some of the same conditions that contribute to the current disarray and lack of effective political response. They include the diffusion of issue focus, the demise of traditional group-issue relationships, and the decrease in the importance of political parties in American political life.

First, there is no major dominant issue concern or set of closely related issues around which an enduring reordering of political allegiances can easily take place. As we have stressed at several points in our discussion, there has been a shift in major policy or issue focus on the part of the citizenry, but a shift that has resulted in several different issues areas about which large segments of the public are concerned. There does not seem to be any major issue or combinations of issues that can weld together a mass electoral coalition on a long-range basis, in the manner in which the issues of economic security and industrial regulation did in the 1930s. To some extent each of the different contemporary issue areas has its own constituency. These constituencies are not necessarily closely related to each other. Persons particularly concerned about race relations may not be those most concerned about the involvement in Southeast Asia. Those who share a common position with respect to the morality of American involvement in Vietnam do not necessarily share common outlooks on how to combat rising crime rates. It is possible, of course, that one major issue area will come to dominate the political agenda or that more congruence between positions on various issues will develop. Data from the 1970 SRC survey suggest a greater congruence between opinions on Vietnam, public order issues, and governmental trust within the mass public in 1970 than had been evident in 1968.

Concern and focus are likely to remain diffuse for some time to come. It seems likely that, at least in the short run, focus on the newer issues will not have force enough either to finally shatter the remnants of the New Deal coalitions or to pull together a new set of electoral coalitions. Without some major crisis a rapid and fundamental restructuring of the electorate seems unlikely.

The lack of a dominant issue focus is compounded by an additional factor, one that also has been a central theme in our discussion. This is the decomposition of much of the group basis of policy preferences. Political coalitions are based, to varying degrees, either on dominant issue concerns or on basic population groupings. In most instances they have entailed a combination of the two. When political preferences are closely tied with group identities, the issue positions and group identities work together to mutually reinforce political allegiances. The working-class Catholic with liberal ideas on social welfare issues in the 1930s was tied into the Democratic party, not only on the basis of his welfare policy preferences, but also because the Democratic party was both the party of the working man and the party to which most of his fellow Catholics belonged. The working-class and Catholic identifications served as important political reference points which tied him into the Democratic party. Even as he moved up the economic ladder, the Catholic identification and the strong association between Catholics and the Democratic party often remained and helped maintain the Democratic preference.

If our picture of contemporary public opinions and the factors that structure them is correct, neither common dominant issue preferences nor policy relevant group affiliations are currently available as forces to successfully move large numbers of voters from one set of allegiances and weld together new enduring political coalitions. In 1972 Nixon was able to appeal to many industrial workers on the basis of implicit racial stands and to others on the basis of law and order or Vietnam. Inasmuch as the industrial workers are themselves split on these issues, it is not possible to speak of Nixon as the candidate of the industrial worker in the same sense that it was said in past decades that the Democratic party was the party of the working man. On the other side of the spectrum, McGovern appealed to some business and professional people on the basis of his strong opposition to the Vietnam involvement. However, even if the war were the major dominant political issue, McGovern would not have been the candidate of businessmen or professionals. Businessmen and professionals have been divided over the Vietnam issue in ways not very dissimilar from the public as a whole and from most other groups in the population. There is no distinctive business-professional position on the war issue. Occupational groupings do not serve as important political reference groups on most contemporary political issues, such as the war, race relations, public order, and governmental trust. They have also become less important as reference points for opinions on the traditional welfare state issues.

The existence of central dominant issue concerns around which differences in interests and opinions were related to major social and demographic groupings has facilitated electoral realignments in the past. The absence of either of these conditions hinders the development of major new electoral groupings at the present time. Another factor that is likely to impede the development of new party coalitions is the waning impact of party in political and electoral life. We have in the course of our discussion presented several types of indications that the electorate seems to be less strongly oriented toward parties than was true in the past. There has been a substantial increase, especially among the young, in the proportion of citizens that do not identify with either of the two major parties. There has been an increase in split-ticket voting. The past decade has also seen the proliferation of ideologically or issue-oriented political groups which have sought to influence government and public policy outside the more conventional party and electoral channels. It may be that in contemporary society political parties are not as crucial for providing either the affective or organizational requirements of electoral life. They may not be as important as basic idenification points or as crucial in the organizing of elections. If these assumptions about the waning impact of parties are correct, then one would expect less pressure for the development of new party coalitions.

We are not suggesting that the reorienting or critical realignment of partisan and electoral life is impossible, nor that it is not likely to occur in the long run. Rather we suggest that the rapid realignment or reordering of the electorate is not likely to take place in the immediate future. We would anticipate that, for the short run, American politics will continue under the current conditions of disarray. Issue concerns and policy coalitions are likely to continue to be volatile. Elections will be conducted under the same prevailing party labels and organizations, with different elections and different campaigns reflecting different short-run concerns and uneasy policy-oriented coalitions.

Notes

[1] The somewhat awkward term *destructured* is used here to convey the notion that there were a series of conditions that structured political opinions and that opinions are no longer structured by those factors, nor do they appear to be structured systematically by any new conditions.

[2] Robert E. Lane, "The Politics of Consensus in an Age of Affluence," *The American Political Science Review* LIX (December 1965), pp. 874–895. This argument was discussed in Chapter 2.

[3] For a good discussion of the makeup of the New Deal coalitions see Samuel Lubell, *The Future of American Politics* (Garden City, N.Y.: Doubleday, 1956).

[4] See Angus Campbell, Philip Converse, Warren Miller, and Donald Stokes, *The American Voter* (New York: Wiley, 1960), for an analysis of voting that emphasizes the use of group identities in partisan preferences and voting decisions.

[5] See, for example, Kevin P. Philips, *The Emerging Republican Majority* (Garden City, N.Y.: Doubleday, 1970), and Richard Scammon and Ben Wattenberg, *The Real Majority* (New York: Coward-McCann, 1970), for two works that take different positions on the contemporary party realignment question.

[6] The concepts of "critical elections" and "secular realignment" have become central ideas in the analysis of American elections and party development. For an early elaboration of these ideas see V. O. Key, Jr., "A Theory of Critical Elections," *Journal of Politics*, 17 (February 1955), pp. 3–18; and V. O. Key, Jr., "Secular Realignment and the Party System," *Journal of Politics*, 21 (May 1959), pp. 198–210. For a more recent and more extensive discussion of critical elections and their role in American politics see Walter Dean Burnham, *Critical*

Elections and the Mainsprings of American Politics (New York: Norton, 1970).
[7] For example, the Free Soil and Know-Nothing parties preceded the Civil War realignment in the mid-nineteenth century; the Populist party of the early 1890s preceded the 1896 sectionalist realignment; and the Progressive party in 1924 hinted at the New Deal realignment of the 1930s.

APPENDIX A
SURVEY RESEARCH

This book is an analysis of the distribution of political opinions in contemporary American society. The arguments and interpretation are based, in large part, on the analysis of public opinion data gathered over the past three and a half decades. Throughout much of the text survey data are presented to make points and to support arguments. Since most of the description and analysis rests upon the use and inter- pretation of survey data, a brief statement on the nature of survey research seems useful. This appendix is designed to provide a brief description of survey research and to identify the sources of the survey data used in the analysis. Appendix B contains a brief explanation of the techniques used to indicate opinion distributions and the degree of association between variables, a form of analysis that is basic to important segments of the analysis of the book. The statement is designed to provide only a very rudimentary description of this important mode of social research.[1]

The measurement of the opinions and preferences of large publics is a common and well-publicized practice in modern society. Public opinion polls that attempt to predict election outcomes are popular and controversial subjects of discussion, especially around the time of presidential elections. Surveys are conducted regularly to ascertain potential markets for consumer products and to learn about citizen plans for spending and saving, as well as to identify public sentiments on public policies and activities of government. The use of survey research in the area of business and marketing, in economic analysis and projections, in learning about social attitudes and behavior, and in ascertaining the policy preferences and voting intentions of the electorate has become a major component of American life. In addition to numerous local and ad hoc surveys there are a number of national survey organizations which do periodic surveys of the American public as a whole.[2] The best known of these is the Gallup Poll. The surveys most often used in the analysis of American voting behavior are those done by the Survey Research Center of the University of Michigan.

Data from these two organizations are used in this analysis.

The widespread use of survey research and the development of public opinion polling as a systematic technique have occurred only over the past four decades. Much of the initial impetus for this development seems to have come from the area of marketing research. The method, however, was very rapidly picked up as a tool for ascertaining political and social preferences. Both the Gallup Poll, conducted by the American Institute of Public Opinion, and The Fortune Survey (or Roper Poll) were begun in 1935. The Gallup Poll made its first presidential election forecasts in 1936. The victory of Roosevelt over Landon was accurately predicted.

Survey research conducted on large populations involves two basic measurement or research tasks. An understanding of these is essential for the comprehension of survey research. First, surveys are generally conducted on some type of *sample* of the population under scrutiny, rather than on the entire population. The designation of an appropriate sample is a crucial factor in survey research. Second, the research involves the identification or measurement of particular preferences, outlooks, and characteristics of those persons who are designated as part of the sample. This is generally accomplished through the *administration of a questionnaire or interview schedule.* The use of scientific survey research occurred simultaneously with the development of sampling theory and of techniques for attitude and opinion measurement.

In most instances in which surveys are carried out it is impossible or impractical to interview all persons in the population under investigation. For example, the administration of an interview to all adult Americans is not feasible in most circumstances. Consequently, it is necessary to use a sample of the population to represent all adult citizens. One seeks responses from a smaller number of individuals who are selected in such a way that one can presume that they represented the significant elements in the larger population. Gallup, the Survey Research Center, and most national surveys currently use samples of between 1,500 and 2,000 persons whose opinions and characteristics they assume are representative of those in the adult population. That is, they select those to be interviewed in such a way to assure that the sample contains numbers of persons in various racial, economic,

geographic, age, religious, political groupings, and so forth, in proportions equal to what exist in the whole population. Approximately 11
percent of adult Americans are black. A good representative sample
would be expected to have approximately 11 percent blacks.
Democrats and Republicans should appear in the sample in the same
proportions that they appear in the population under investigation.

Samples of a given population can be drawn in a variety of ways.
They can vary considerably in size. The crucial criteria for a good
sample is that it be representative. It should not overrepresent some
elements of the population and underrepresent others. Trying to assure
that a sample does not contain some sort of bias, or overrepresentation
of some elements of the population, is more crucial than the number of
persons appearing in the sample. Gallup polls have been fairly accurate
in predicting the outcomes of national elections with samples of only
1,500 respondents. In 1936 the Literary Digest Poll, using a sample of
some 12 million persons, predicted an electoral victory for Alfred
Landon over Franklin Roosevelt. This turned out to be a grossly
inaccurate prediction. The sample used was based upon names taken
from automobile registration lists and telephone directories. Cars and
telephones were both luxury items during the 1930s. The sample
consequently overrepresented the wealthier segments of society, those
who were more likely to vote against Roosevelt. Despite the very large
number of persons appearing in the sample, the systematic bias inherent
in the sample caused a massive misrepresentation of voter intention.[3]
Representativeness, not size in itself, is the crucial element in a good
sample. With respect to the number of interviews used the Gallup
organization reports: "Polling accuracy today is not so much a function
of the number of persons included in a survey as it is upon the proper
selection of these persons. After many years of balancing costs and
other factors against the level of accuracy required, the Gallup Poll
fixed upon 1,500 as the unit best suited for its needs."[4]

Most public opinion polls or sample surveys of large populations use
some type of prepared interview schedule in their efforts to ascertain
the outlooks and characteristics of the public. The major objective of
the survey interview is to obtain responses to a set of common basic
questions from those persons who are part of the sample. Questions
must be uniform, unbiased, and generally comprehensible in order to

elicit comparable and accurate measurements of individual opinions. They can be administered in person by an interviewer who reads the questions and records the responses, or they can be mailed to the respondent, allowing him to fill out the questionnaire on his own and return it to the researcher. Surveys can also be carried out by use of the telephone. For the most part, major survey research organizations use trained interviewers who call on the selected respondents and administer a series of preformulated questions to the interviewees in person.

The length of interview schedules varies. Gallup generally uses a relatively short questionnaire, one that involves a series of background questions and items attempting to ascertain opinions on a few issues. He administers a questionnaire to a national sample on a very regular basis. The Survey Research Center, on the other hand, does very extensive surveys of electoral behavior every two years, in conjunction with national elections. Extensive questionnaires, probing a wide variety of political and social outlooks, as well as basic social and demographic characteristics and policy and candidate preferences, are used in SRC election surveys.

This book is based largely on the analysis of data from national sample surveys conducted by the Survey Research Center of the University of Michigan. Data from their 1968 election survey serve as the core of the analysis. Data from Survey Research Center surveys taken in conjunction with other elections, running from 1956 through 1970, are used upon occasion to add a trend dimension. In order to broaden the analysis and to include opinions not tapped by the SRC surveys, data from Gallup polls (American Institute of Public Opinion surveys) are also used in the discussion and analysis. Data taken from The Survey Research Center studies are generally referred to in the text as SRC data. Gallup poll data are referred to as such or as A.I.P.O. surveys.

With respect to both SRC data and Gallup poll data, when we say that data from a particular study report that a given percentage of respondents favored or opposed a particular issue, we are referring to the responses of a carefully selected sample of between 1,500 and 2,000 persons representing the adult American population. We presume that the distribution of opinions in the population as a whole is the same as that in the sample. In this way the sample survey data indicate distributions in the population with which we are concerned.

Most survey organizations doing surveys of the entire American population use some form of area probability sample, in which counties are the primary sample units. That is, the first step in designating the sample is to draw a random sample of the more than 3,000 counties in the United States. Then, more specific areas within the county, townships, cities, or parts of cities are chosen, usually at random. Finally specific residences are selected within these smaller units, and interviewers are instructed to get interviews from persons in those residences. In this manner samples are drawn which are presumed to be representative of the adult civilian population living in private households. Persons living in prisons, hospitals, religious and educational institutions, and military reservations are generally not included in the samples used for national surveys. Both Gallup and the Survey Research Center use some variation of this method for drawing the samples they use in their surveys. Interviewers with set questionnaires attempt to interview particular individuals living in the specified residences.

We would like to make clear that all of the data used in this analysis were collected by Gallup, the Survey Research Center, or other survey research organizations. None of it was collected by the author or specifically for use in this analysis. The data used in this analysis were made available through two survey data repository and dissemination organizations. The Survey Research Center data were made available through the Inter-University Consortium for Political Research, located at the University of Michigan. Some of the Gallup Poll data and the data from Roper and National Opinion Research Center studies were obtained through the Roper Center International Survey Library Association, located at Williams College. Both of these organizations obtain and make available to scholars and students a vast array of survey research data, some of it going back as far as the mid-1930s when systematic opinion surveying got under way. The work of these organizations in gathering, processing, and disseminating survey research data makes works like this book possible.

Notes

[1] For a more detailed analysis of survey research see Charles H. Backstrum and Gerald D. Hursh, *Survey Research* (Evanston, Ill.: Northwestern University Press, 1963); Herbert Hyman, *Survey Design and Analysis* (New York: Free Press, 1955); Morris H. Hansen, William H. Hurwitz, and William G. Madaw, *Sample Survey Methods and Theory* (New York: Wiley, 1953).

[2] For a brief history of the development of public opinion polling, and of survey research organizations see Bernard Hennessy, *Public Opinion* (Belmont, Calif.: Wadsworth, 1965), especially chapters 1, 2, and 3.

[3] See Hennessy, op. cit., pp. 39–41 and Claude E. Robinson, *Straw Votes: A Study of Political Predicting* (New York: Columbia University Press, 1932).

[4] *The Gallup Opinion Index* No. 59 (Princeton, N.J.: Gallup International, May 1970), p. 17.

APPENDIX B
MEASURES OF DISTRIBUTION
AND ASSOCIATION

The discussion and arguments of this book are built upon the analysis of survey research data. Data from national surveys are presented and discussed at many points in the text to illustrate opinion distributions and to substantiate particular points. A variety of forms of data presentation and statistical analysis are used in the course of the discussion. Since some readers may not be familiar with all of the forms of data presentation and the methods of analysis employed, a brief and elementary description of these methods seems appropriate. That is the objective of this appendix. This description will not involve a technical or detailed account of the techniques used. Rather, the attempt is to offer simple descriptions of the basic methods and to state how and why they are used so that the reader unfamiliar with such techniques will be able to better interpret the arguments of the book.

Two very general exercises in data analyses are employed in the book. One of these is the simple description of response distributions within a given population. A variation of this involves comparisons between distributions among several different populations, the same population at different time points, and between several subgroupings of a particular population. The other general exercise entails the measurement of association between two different factors. For example one may wish to know the extent to which different levels of income are related to different opinions on government welfare spending.

DESCRIPTIONS OF
OPINION DISTRIBUTIONS

Perhaps the most common and basic question one is apt to ask about public opinion data is how opinions with respect to a given issue are distributed within a particular population. Stating it in a more operational way, one asks how answers to a particular question (or maybe a series of questions) are distributed among the respondents to a survey. How many people are for and how many against a particular policy proposal? For the most part, the concerns of this discussion are the political opinions of the adult American population. Methodologically this involves looking at the distributions of responses given to various questions asked of a representative sample of that population.

Let us say that we are interested in opinions respecting government integration efforts. The 1968 Survey Research Center election study asked a sample of the American population whether they thought the federal government should or should not "see to it that white and Negro children are allowed to go to the same schools." (See Table 2.5.) The distribution of responses, among those giving an answer to this question was as follows: 593 said the federal government should; 103 said that it depends; and 681 responded that the government should not. These figures represent the basic distribution of responses to that item. Slightly more respondents felt that the government should not push school integration than thought it should. That relationship is ascertainable from the raw distribution figures.

Interpreting raw figures like these, however, can be somewhat cumbersome. One often seeks a more precise and meaningful notion of the magnitude of support versus opposition on a given issue. The use of raw figures becomes even more of a problem when one tries to compare the distribution of opinions on one issue with the distributions on other issues. In the same 1968 SRC survey a question was asked about support for federal equal public accommodations legislation. In the responses to this item 812 thought the government should be involved in seeing that Negroes have the right to go to any hotel or restaurant they can afford; 517 thought the government in Washington should stay out of this matter; 38 said it depends. The raw figures indicating responses to each of the two racial items give an indication of whether more people supported or opposed government action in each of the two racial issues. They do not, however, provide an easily interpreted and precise comparison between the two distributions. It is not easy to ascertain from these raw figures just how the level of support for government involvement in school integration compares to the level of support for public accommodations.

The conversion of the raw figures into percentages often is used as a means of obtaining a single measure of distribution that is more properly interpretable and that allows more meaningful comparisons between two or more distributions. The conversion of raw figures into percentages involves the reduction of the series of absolute figures into a standard numerical base, one that is more compatible with the habit of thinking in terms of decimals. Thus the three individual raw figures in each distribution can be converted into their relationship to parts of one hundred. After converting the two sets of responses into percentages, we can say that 43 percent of the respondents favored government action with respect to school integration and 59 percent favored government action with respect to public accommodations; 50 percent opposed school integration efforts and 38 percent opposed public accommodation action. With percentages we have an easily perceived and accurate measurement of the relative level of support for school integration versus public accommodation efforts, only 43 out of every 100 favored school desegregation efforts. In most instances when opinion distributions or comparative distributions are used in the text, percentages or relative frequencies are presented.

Percentages also are used for two other exercises in this text. Often one is interested in knowing what happens to opinion distributions on a particular issue over some span of time. If the same question is asked of the same population, or a series of representative samples of the same population, over a number of time points it is possible to compare the distributions of responses to those items and get a picture of whether opinions have altered or remained stable over that time span. Again, the computation of percentages from the raw figures facilitates the comparison of the several distributions by norming the different figures to a comparable base. For example, Table 2.3 shows changes in opinions regarding the Vietnam involvement over a six-year period, from 1964 to 1970. In each of the three surveys the question asked was: "Do you think we did the right thing in getting into the fighting in Vietnam or should we have stayed out?" (See Table 2.3.) The data show that in 1964, 60 percent of the respondents reported holding that the right thing had been done in getting involved in Vietnam. In 1968,

36 percent took that position. In 1970, 38 percent thought we had
done the right thing. The use of percentages allows one to readily see
the shift in opinions from 1964 to 1968 and the relative stability of
opinions between 1968 and 1970.

Time series data based on percentages also can be presented in
graph form, as in Figure 2.5. The graph is based on data from a series of
Gallup Poll questions posed at six-month intervals, which asked
whether or not the respondent thought that the Vietnam involvement
had been a mistake. The graph line indicates changes over time, from
1965 to 1971, in the percentage of respondents indicating that the
involvement had been a mistake. This line allows one to grasp visually
the substantial shift that occurred over that six-year time span. The
data points at each of the half-year intervals represent the percentage of
respondents saying that a mistake had been made. From this graph one
can readily see, not only the overall change, but also the amount and
direction of change within shorter time spans. For example, the graph
shows that the sharpest decrease in support for the involvement
occurred between the spring and fall of 1967.

One of the major concerns of this book is how various social,
economic, demographic, and political conditions structure differences
in political opinions. Stating this in another form: to what extent do
persons in different income, occupational, racial, age, and partisan
groupings tend to differ in their political outlooks? Do wealthier
citizens tend to support government involvement in integration efforts
in higher proportions than poorer citizens? Are younger people more
likely to support government welfare expenditures than older people?
One of the ways to look at these issues is to compare the distributions
of opinions on a given issue within several particular population
subgroupings. For example, if we are interested in whether people in
different occupational groupings vary in their level of support for
day-care centers, we can divide the population (sample) into different
occupational groupings, compute percentages of support for day-care
centers within each of the occupational categories, and compare these
percentages with each other. This is a technique we use extensively in
this book. The level of support within six major occupational categories
for day-care centers is shown in Figure 4.2. The data are presented in a
series of bar graphs to add a visual dimension to the presentation. The

figures at the top of each bar indicate the percent of persons within that particular occupational category who replied that they supported government expenditures for day-care centers. These figures indicate strong levels of support for day-care centers within all occupational groupings, except for farmers. They indicate the highest levels of support came from professional and clerical and sales persons, followed by nonskilled workers, skilled workers, business managers, and farmers in that order. Except for the farmers there are not very great differences in the level of support for day-care centers among the several occupational groupings.

This method for comparing the relative distributions of opinions among particular population subgroupings is employed with respect to geographical divisions, age, race, political participation, and party attachment as well as for occupational groupings. In most instances the data are presented in the form of bar graphs like those discussed above.

The computation of percentages is the most widely used statistical technique employed in the manipulation and presentation of data in this book. It is an easily comprehensible technique, one with which most readers are likely to be familiar. It is very useful for the investigation and presentation of data with respect to many of the questions pertaining to the description and comparison of opinion distributions which are the central concerns of the arguments developed in the book.

MEASURES OF STATISTICAL ASSOCIATION

The other general methodological exercise used in this book is the measurement of association between two different factors. One of the central features of developing descriptions and explanations about social behavior is the search for patterns of relationship or association. We seek to ascertain whether the existence of one behavior tends to occur in relationship to the existence of another behavior or condition, or whether more of one factor varies with more or less of another factor. For example, we may want to describe or explain liberal attitudes with respect to social welfare spending. We want to know something more than what the distribution of welfare attitudes is within a given population. We want to know what other attitudes or conditions may be related to liberal or conservative attitudes on welfare. We can investigate, for example, whether or not variations in the level of incomes are associated with variations of opinions on welfare. Do persons in higher-income levels tend to be more conservative on social welfare issues than people with lower levels of income?

These types of issues are central to much of the investigation of questions concerning political behavior and of public opinion. We seek to ascertain patterns of covariation, instances where one factor (an opinion, for example) is likely to vary or occur in relationship to another factor (a social-economic or demographic condition, for example). Two broad types of issues or questions fall under these general considerations. On the one hand, there is the question of simple joint occurrence. Is one factor likely to be present when another factor is? On the other hand, there is the question of parallel changes in two or more factors. Is an increase in one factor likely to be associated with an increase in another factor? In this book the emphasis is on the latter type of relationship. Where we attempt to measure statistically the level of association between two factors, we are concerned with the extent to which an increase or decrease of one factor is associated, in an orderly way, with an increase or decrease of another factor.

There are a number of statistical techniques that can be used in the measurement of levels of association. To a considerable degree such techniques must be adapted to the nature of the data as well as the substantive concerns. Measures of statistical association are employed in this text in instances where both of the factors under consideration are measured in terms of ordinal or rank order indicators—that is, variables in which the individual respondents can be placed on a continuum in which each response category can be identified as a greater or lesser degree of a particular attribute. For example, with respect to income categories it is possible to place individuals in some sort of rank order which indicates that the individuals have higher or lower incomes in comparison with persons who fall at other points in the measurement scale. A person with a $5,000 per year income would be placed above those with less than $5,000 per year and below those individuals whose incomes are above $5,000 per year. When these types of judgments can be made, one can claim to have a rank order or an ordinal scale.

Several types of statistical measures of association are applicable to ordinal scales. Gamma is the statistical measure used in this book. It is a measure widely used in the social sciences.[1] It measures the extent to which it is possible to predict the order along one variable from the order on the other variable. To what extent, for example, is it possible to predict opinions on welfare issues on the basis of knowing something about income level? Gamma scores can range from -1 to +1. A score of 0.0 would indicate a lack of association between the two variables. Scores ranging from .0 to +1.0 indicate that the two variables are positively related—that is, an increase along one variable is related to an increase along the other variable. The higher the score, the closer to +1.0, and the further from 0.0, the stronger the level of association, or the higher the percentage of reduction of prediction errors in predicting order along one variable from order on the other. Minus or negative coefficients indicate an inverse relationship between the variables: the higher the score along one variable the lower the position along the other. The same range and interpretation of range from .0 to -1.0 is applicable for both negative and positive relationships. A gamma of .45 would indicate a stronger level of association than a gamma of .21. A gamma of .004 would indicate virtually no ordered association between two variables.

Notes

[1] For a discussion of gamma as a measure of association see John H. Mueller, Karl F. Schuessler, and Herbert L. Costner, *Statistical Reasoning in Sociology* (Boston: Houghton Mifflin, 1970), pp. 279–294.

INDEX

DATE DUE

MAY ~~noon~~			
GAYLORD			PRINTED IN U.S A.

73 74 75 76 77 9 8 7 6 5 4 3 2 1